For Christ's Sake

Part One of
the *Revised Edition*
of *Blood on the Cross*

Ahmad Thomson and

Muhammad 'Ata'ur-Rahim

Ta-Ha Publishers Ltd.
1 Wynne Road
London SW9 0BB
United Kingdom

© Jumada al-Awwal 1417/October 1996 Ahmad Thomson

First Edition published by Ta-Ha Publishers Ltd in 1989 in the form of the first half of *Blood on the Cross*.

Revised Edition published by:

Ta-Ha Publishers Ltd
1 Wynne Road
London SW9 0BB

Revised and typeset by Ahmad Thomson.

British Library Cataloguing in Publication Data
Thomson, Ahmad
For Christ's Sake
1. Christianity – Europe   2. Europe – Church history
I. Title II. 'Ata'ur-Rahim, M.

ISBN 1 897940 51 3

Printed by Deluxe Printers, London.

Contents

By the Same Authors

Islam in Andalus – Part Two of the *Revised Edition*
of *Blood on the Cross*, 1996.

Jesus, Prophet of Islam – *Revised Edition*, 1996.

'If you would divine the future, study the past.'

Confucius

Preface
to the
Revised Edition

Most of what is recorded in the pages which follow was originally written between 1977 and 1979 and was the result of the joint efforts of Colonel Muhammad 'Ata'ur-Rahim, *alehi rahma*, and myself. Having already worked together on *Jesus, Prophet of Islam* between 1975 and 1977, we had become accustomed to working together as a team, and shortly after *Jesus, Prophet of Islam* was completed, Colonel Rahim and I began work on another book, this time on the history of Islam in Spain. To our delight, it turned out to be a natural progression of the work which we had already been doing together, for it soon became clear that the history of Islam in Spain could only be fully understood if the reader was first presented with a brief history of how the religion of Christianity had developed in Europe, especially as regards the interaction between the Unitarian Christians and the Trinitarian Christians.

The first draft of this book – which dealt principally with the history of Christianity in Europe – was completed shortly before I departed on a six month journey whose objective and high-point was to do the *hajj* in Makka and to visit the Prophet Muhammad, may Allah bless him and grant him peace, who is buried in Madina. Not long after my return to England, Colonel Rahim died peacefully in his sleep, in 1978, and was subsequently buried in Brookwood cemetery, near Woking, may he have peace in his grave. Accordingly the last third of the book, which concentrated mainly on the history of the Muslims in Spain was written after his death.

Although the book was completed in 1979, it was not until 1989 that it came to be printed, under the title *Blood on the Cross*, in an edited form which was considered necessary to avoid having a book which was 'too long', and which I had not had the opportunity to examine or approve, and with which I was not subsequently entirely happy. Although many of the changes to the original text which appeared in the first edition of *Blood on the Cross* did indeed generally improve the text, especially as regards style and clarity

of expression, certain passages were removed which, in my opinion – and I believe Colonel Rahim would have agreed with me –
should have remained, and perhaps would have remained had the
editors also been involved in the lengthy research which had both
preceded and accompanied the writing of the book.

Although the first edition of the book was, on the whole, well
received, one of the main criticisms which did come from more
than one quarter was that it was really two books in one – one on
the history of Christianity in Europe, and one on the history of
Islam in Spain. Furthermore, it was pointed out, the reader was
often only really interested in one of these 'two' books, but not in
both of them, and accordingly it was irksome to have to wade
through material which therefore appeared unnecessary. It is with
this criticism in mind, and out of a desire to restore some of the
passages which were edited out of the original text without my
knowledge or permission, that the revised edition of *Blood on the
Cross* has accordingly now been divided into two books. Hopefully those who wish to understand the nature of the interaction
between Christianity and Islam in Europe more fully will read both!

The first book, entitled *For Christ's Sake*, deals principally with
the history of Christianity in Europe, with particular reference to
Spain. The second book, entitled *Islam in Andalus* – which was the
title originally chosen by Colonel Rahim and myself for the original book – deals principally with the history of the Muslims in
Spain. Both books contain passages which were edited out of the
original work, and both books contain additional material which
has come to light during the last seventeen years – another reason
why a revised edition has been considered necessary.

In presenting these two revised editions to the general public, I
hope not only that Colonel Rahim would approve of these changes
if he were here to see them, but also that whoever reads them will
learn something of value from them and will, above all, enjoy them.
I certainly enjoyed writing much of them with Colonel Rahim, and
it has been a pleasure to revise the original text after so many years,
reminding me as it has of what a very human human being Colonel Rahim was. Colonel Rahim's warmth and wisdom were extraordinary, and many of the long discussions which we shared
and his sharp observations are still with me today.

Anyone who ever had the good fortune to meet Colonel Rahim
will remember him with deep affection. He was what his name
indicated – a gift from a Compassionate Lord – and these two re-

vised editions are dedicated to his memory. May we meet again in the next world, in the Garden!

As with any book written by a human being, there are inevitably shortcomings and deficiencies in this, the first of the two books, *For Christ's Sake*. Thousands of pages have been read in order that tens may be written. Hopefully this book will nevertheless complement the knowledge which the reader already possesses, giving fresh insight into what may have been unknown, or half-forgotten, or too readily assumed.

It should perhaps be emphasised that the title of this book is not intended to be provocative. One of the criticisms that is often levelled at 'religion' in general is that it preaches peace and love but results in turmoil and bloodshed. It would appear, however, that it is an essential part of human nature to fight for *whatever* one firmly believes in, whatever that may be, and that this holds true for all religions – both those which are the corruptions of earlier prophetic teachings as well as those which are entirely man-made – whether they be the religions of Judaism, or Christianity, or Islam, for example, or the religions of making money, or establishing democracy, or building empires.

At one time or another, both wonderful and terrible things have been done in the name of various great men, and with all the sincerity and commitment in the world. What has been done in the name of Jesus is no exception: Some of the most exquisite musical compositions and some of the bloodiest massacres, for example, have been done 'for Christ's sake' and with the intention of either attaining purity or maintaining purity – although as most people are being made increasingly aware nowadays, purity and orthodoxy are not necessarily or always synonymous with each other.

Finally, I would like to thank my guide and teacher, Shaykh Abdal-Qadir al-Murabit, for it was through him that I came to embrace Islam, and it was thanks to him that I came to work with Colonel Rahim, and it was at his suggestion that Colonel Rahim and I began to explore the history of Islam in Spain. *Al-hamdulillahi wa shukrulillah wa la howla wa la quwwata ila bi'llah* – Praise belongs to Allah and thanks belongs to Allah and there is no power and no strength except from Allah. And, as the Prophet Muhammad said, may Allah bless him and grant him peace, 'If you do not thank people – then you have not thanked Allah.'

Ahmad Thomson
London 1416/1995

Acknowledgements

My thanks are especially due to my guide and teacher, Shaykh 'Abd al-Qadir al-Murabit who originally suggested that this book be written, and to Colonel Muhammad Ata'ur-Rahim who helped every step of the way, not only by assisting with the research work in the British Museum Library and by listening to and commenting on what had been written as it was written, but also by giving me food and shelter for much of the time. About a third of the book was written after Colonel Rahim's death, may he have peace in his grave, and soon after it was completed he appeared in a clear dream, smiling, and said, 'Did you know that I was with you all the time you were writing it!' My thanks are also due to the *fuqara'* who benefited us with their company while the book was being written, to Hajj 'Abdal-Haqq Bewley and Hajj Idris Mears for their help in editing and typesetting the first edition, to Aisha Bewley for typing the manuscript, and to Afsar Siddiqui, who has always encouraged and helped me, for publishing it. I am indebted to you for everything I have learned from you during the extraordinary time spent in your company. Time passes, things change, but memories remain. May Allah give you all great *baraka* in this world and in the Next World. Amin.

Preface
to the
First Edition

Blood on the Cross outlines the history of that extraordinary period during which the Muslims flourished and perished in southern Spain. It was largely due to their presence and illumination in the Iberian peninsula that the Dark Ages in Europe came to an end, and their influence is still with us today in a thousand ways.

In order to fully realise how it was that the Muslims in Spain came to be almost completely eliminated by the notorious Spanish Inquisition, the book begins with an outline of the history of what is today called Christianity, tracing the movement of the original Unitarian followers of Jesus, peace be upon him, from North Africa and the Middle East into Europe and southern Spain, describing the formation and expansion of the Trinitarian church in Italy and the rest of Europe, and outlining the almost total annihilation of the Unitarian Christians at the hands of the Trinitarian church by means of the Mediaeval and Spanish Inquisitions.

Without this analysis of the interaction between the Unitarian and Trinitarian Christians, it is virtually impossible to understand how it was that the inhabitants of the Iberian peninsula in the eighth century AD embraced Islam so readily and rapidly, and how it was that the Jews and the Muslims of Spain in the sixteenth century were either exterminated by the Spanish Inquisition or forced to flee for their lives. What took place in Spain during the intervening centuries is fascinating. Anyone who is aware of what happened in the Iberian peninsula between 711 and 1609 AD will understand why Spain is the way it is today.

It is accepted by all Muslims and some Unitarian Christians that Jesus, peace be upon him, was not crucified and is not the son of God. The creation of Jesus was like the creation of Adam, peace be upon them: **'When God wishes something to exist, He says, "Be!" and it is.'** To these Unitarians, Jesus is a Messenger of God who confirmed the teachings of Moses and foretold of the coming of Muhammad, may the blessings and peace of Allah be upon them and their families and their companions and all their followers. The Trinitarian Christians – who have somehow mistakenly sought to affirm that Jesus was and is simultaneously a human being, the son of God and God Himself, but who nevertheless prayed to and worshipped God and was crucified – have always, as the historical record so clearly demonstrates, waged war both ideologically and physically on whoever affirmed the Unitarian view, whether they were Jews, Christians or Muslims.

Blood on the Cross is part of that historical record. This book is, however, intended for anyone who likes to read about other peoples in other places in other times, whatever their own beliefs or perceptions of existence may be, as well as for serious students of the history of Christianity and Islam and Europe who may wish to consult the books listed in the bibliography in order to arrive at an understanding which is far greater than this book can contain. May you enjoy it, and find whatever you seek!

Ahmad Thomson
Dhu'l-Hijjah 1409

Introduction

The Muslims – who in the present context are usually referred to as 'the Moors' – were in Spain for over eight hundred years. In many areas, especially in the south, which today still retains its ancient name of Andalucia, or Andalus, they formed an overwhelming majority of the population. Islam flowered and flourished in the land in a light which diminished the shadows of the Dark Ages in Europe, and which cast illumination where before there was only ignorance. As long as they remained established in the worship of their Creator, the Muslims of Andalus enjoyed a quality of life unparalleled in the rest of Europe:

> Europe was darkened at sunset, Cordova shone with public lamps; Europe was dirty, Cordova built a thousand baths; Europe was covered with vermin, Cordova changed its undergarments daily; Europe lay in mud, Cordova's streets were paved; Europe's palaces had smoke-holes in the ceiling, Cordova's arabesques were exquisite; Europe's nobility could not sign its name, Cordova's children went to school; Europe's monks could not read the baptismal service, Cordova's teachers created a library of Alexandrian dimensions. [1]

Today the Muslims' presence in Spain is virtually non-existent. Similarly, the Jews who once formed an influential and important minority during the period of Muslim rule have almost completely disappeared from Spain. There is no longer any trace of the Goths who were Unitarians by conviction, and who once ruled over Italy, southern France and Spain. Similarly, the Unitarian Christians who were known as the Paulicians and who came after the Goths, no longer exist in these countries.

The Muslims, the Jews, the Goths and the Paulicians all had one fundamental belief in common: They all affirmed that there is only One God. They were hated by the Roman Catholic Church because of this, and during different stages in the history of Spain they were systematically persecuted and massacred in the Name of God by this institution, and most of their books were destroyed.

* * * * *

An understanding of the basic pattern of the Trinitarian persecution of those who believed in the Divine Unity is essential for anyone who wishes to remove the dust and whitewash which up to now have liberally obscured the history of Spain. The history of Islam in Andalus – which is the name by which the Iberian peninsula was and still is known to the Muslims – cannot be understood without examining the nature of this pattern, for the Roman Catholic persecution of the Muslims in Spain was not an isolated event, but an extension of the earlier persecution of the Christian Unitarians and of the Jews.

It is therefore necessary to discover how it was that the Roman Catholic Church came to believe that it was 'lawful' to torture and kill the 'heretic' and burn his books – for Christ's sake – 'heretic' being the appellation attached to anyone who disagreed with the Roman Catholic Church. Thus in order to view the history of Islam in Andalus in its true perspective it is necessary to first examine the early history of Christianity, and to see how Roman Catholic beliefs and policies first arose.

Chapter One

The Nazarenes
and the
Christians

Jesus, peace be upon him, started his mission when he was thirty
years old. It did not last more than three years. He left behind him
the twelve Apostles, seventy disciples and a large following in the
rural area of Judea. These villages, or the *Am Al-Arez* as they were
called, formed the majority of the population. Drawn by the wisdom and the miracles of Jesus, they gathered round him and followed him. They recognised the light which re-illuminated the
teaching which Moses had brought before, and which Jesus had
come to clarify and revivify:

> Jesus's mission was solely to establish worship of the
> Creator in the manner in which He had ordained. He
> and his followers were prepared to fight anyone who
> tried to prevent them from living as their Lord wished
> them to. [1]

Many of the priests of the Temple used their position as a means to
wealth and reputation. They were not happy either with the per-
ceptive remarks of Jesus which revealed their hypocrisy, or with
the popularity which Jesus had acquired amongst the common people which threatened their status. The Romans who were ruling
Judea, regarded the emergence of this new leader with increasing
suspicion, fearing it could result in another revolt of the Jews. They
had already had enough trouble from the Essenes, the dwellers of
the caves round the Dead Sea. This group of the Jewish community refused to accept the Roman customs and laws where they
conflicted with the teachings of Moses. They were dedicated to
maintaining the purity of their way of life and to freeing Judea
from foreign occupation. Along with their daily prayers and study

of the Scriptures, many of them practised the martial arts. The members of this fighting force were called *Zealots*. It is probable that Jesus spent much of his childhood amongst the Essenes, not only by the Dead Sea, but also near Alexandria where they had another colony. Many of them subsequently became his followers. This annoyed the priests even further.

Thus the Roman rulers and the corrupt priests of the Temple discovered a common interest against Jesus and his followers. It was the conspiracy hatched between them which culminated in the disappearance of Jesus and the crucifixion of another man, probably Judas Iscariot, 'that he might suffer that horrible death to which he had sold another.' [2] The mistaken belief, so ardently adopted by Paul of Tarsus, that it was Jesus who was crucified, was one of the first causes of schism in the early Church:

> Those disciples who did not fear God went by night and stole the body of Judas and hid it, spreading a report that Jesus was risen again; whence great confusion arose. The high priest then commanded, under pain of Anathema, that no one should talk of Jesus of Nazareth. And so there arose a great persecution, and many were stoned and many beaten, and many banished from the land, because they could not hold their peace on such a matter. [3]

The persecution of the followers of Jesus, not only by the Romans, but also by the Jews who had rejected Jesus, was another major cause of schism in the early Church. One of the more enthusiastic of the Jewish persecutors was Saul of Tarsus, the 'Hebrew of the Hebrews', who later became famous as Paul. He pursued his task with vigour and efficiency as he himself admitted:

> You have heard ... how that beyond measure I persecuted the Church of God and wasted it – and profited in the Jews' religion above many of my equals in mine own nation, being more exceedingly zealous of the traditions of my fathers. (*Galatians 1: 13-15*).

The persecution by the Jews and the Romans strengthened some but discouraged others. The weaker followers compromised their beliefs and their actions to avoid it, and, on account of this, contradictions and disputes amongst the followers of Jesus arose.

It was Paul, once again, who played a large part in this process of compromise which inevitably blurred the purity of the way of life which Jesus had brought. With dramatic suddenness he announced that he had seen Jesus in a vision and had decided to become his follower. However, he waited three years in Arabia and Damascus before returning to Jerusalem to inform the Apostles of this miraculous occurrence. They were now known as Nazarenes. They had been closest to Jesus when he was on earth and were not convinced about the genuineness of Paul's conversion. Their scepticism increased when Paul, who had never sat with Jesus, began to preach a doctrine which differed from, and often contradicted, what they had heard from Jesus himself. Paul later justified his position by saying:

> I certify you brethren that the Gospel which was preached of me is not after man. For I neither received it of man, neither was I taught it, but by the revelation of Jesus Christ. (*Galatians 1: 11-12*).

However, the Nazarenes must have found it impossible to believe that Jesus, having trained his twelve Apostles to spread his teaching while on earth would then, from the Unseen, supersede their authority and change his original teaching without informing them, and by means of a man who had never even met him. Paul's arguments carried little weight with James, the head of the Nazarenes in Jerusalem. It is not clear whether James was the son of Mary by Joseph or the son of Mary's sister. It is known that he was very close to Jesus and according to the New Testament he was one of the more active and outspoken of the Apostles. Jesus gave him and John the name of *Boanerges* – Sons of Thunder. According to Eusebius he spent so much time praying in intercession for people that his knees grew as horny as those of a camel. Due to his sincerity and honesty he became known as James the Just. He is regarded as being the first bishop of Jerusalem, although this title was not used at that time. He was one of the most respected people in Jerusalem, and it was to him that many appeals were made to curb Paul's tongue, and to silence his new doctrine of Christ. He was the central figure in the controversy between Paul and the Apostles. [4]

It is possible that Paul may well have been completely rejected by the Nazarenes who still remembered his part in their persecution. It was only due to the influence of Barnabas that Paul was finally accepted into their community. Perhaps Barnabas felt that Paul would adopt their way of life through keeping company with the people who had directly learned so much from Jesus. However, Paul, who realised that he had been accepted into their midst because of Barnabas's support and not because of his own merits, did not stay with them but returned to Tarsus in anger.

Many of the closest followers of Jesus had gone to Antioch to escape persecution by the Jews and the Romans. Barnabas eventually joined them and became the leader of the growing Nazarene community there. They held firmly to the pattern of life which Jesus had embodied. They began to accept people who were not Jews into their number. It was at about this time that the world 'Christian' came into usage. It was used as a term of ridicule and abuse, rather than of description.

A stage was reached where Barnabas decided to take the message of Jesus further afield. He went to Tarsus and brought Paul back with him to Antioch. Thus for the second time Paul came face to face with the people he had once persecuted. He received the same cool reception from the disciples in Antioch as he had experienced from them in Jerusalem. There was a bitter controversy between them concerning not only what Jesus had taught, but also to whom it should be taught. Again it was only thanks to Barnabas that Paul was accepted into their number. Finally Barnabas and Paul, accompanied by Mark, the son of Barnabas's sister, set off for Greece on their first missionary journey.

For a Jew whose heart was receptive it was an easy matter to accept Jesus whose teaching only served to illuminate a pattern of life with which he was already familiar. For a Gentile, to whom the ways of the Jews were strange and often despised, it was difficult. The Greeks worshipped a myriad of gods. They did not mind increasing the number of gods, but opposed the affirmation of the Divine Unity which negated any other object of worship.

It soon became evident that Paul was prepared to compromise the teaching of Jesus in order to make it acceptable to them. Barnabas could not bear with this. It is recorded in *Acts 15: 39-40* that, 'the contention was so sharp between them, that they departed asunder one from the other – and so Barnabas took Mark and sailed unto Cyprus,' which was Barnabas's birth-place.

Paul then travelled west with Peter. Without the sincerity of Barnabas or the counsel of those who followed Jesus to restrain him, he must have met with little opposition to his new doctrines and adapted ways of conduct and behaviour. Paul deviated further and further away from the teaching Jesus had embodied, and laid more and more emphasis on the figure of Christ whom he claimed had appeared to him in visions. His teaching relied entirely on supernatural communication, and not on any historical testimony of a living Jesus. His defence against those who accused him of changing the guidance Jesus had brought was that what he preached had its origin in a direct revelation to him from Christ, and as such had Divine Authority. It was by virtue of this 'authority' he claimed, that the blessings of the Gospel were not limited to the Jews, but to all who believed. Furthermore he asserted that the requirements of the law of Moses were not only unnecessary but also contrary to what had been directly revealed to him from God. In fact, he said, referring to *Deuteronomy 21: 23* in the process, they were a curse:

> Christ redeemed us from the curse of the law by becoming a curse for us, for it is written: 'Cursed is everyone who is hanged on a tree.' (*Galatians 3: 13*).

Thus Paul incurred not only the anger of the followers of Jesus but also that of the Jews since he was contradicting both of their Prophets and all the Prophets before them. It is clear why he chose to spread his teaching amongst people who hated the Jews and who had not heard about Jesus from any one else's lips.

Paul justified his new doctrine with the use of this analogy:

> Know ye not, brethren, (for I speak to them that know the law) how that the law hath dominion over a man as long as he liveth? For the woman which hath an husband is bound by the law to her husband so long as he liveth; but if the husband be dead, she is loosed from the law of her husband. So then, if, while her husband liveth, she be married to another man, she shall be called an adulteress: but, if her husband be dead, she is free from that law, so that she is no adulteress, though she be married to another man. Wherefore, my brethren, ye also are become dead to the law by the body of Christ;

that ye should be married to another, even to him who
is raised from the dead, that we should bring forth fruit
unto God. (*Romans* 7: 1-4).

The use of this analogy clearly indicates that Paul made a distinction between Jesus and 'Christ'. According to his reasoning, the
law which had bound Jesus and his followers was no longer necessary, since Jesus had died. Now they were no longer 'married' to
Jesus, but to Christ, who had brought another law. It was, therefore, necessary to follow Christ and not Jesus. Thus, anyone who
still persisted in holding to Jesus's original teaching had gone astray.
    Paul himself was not altogether clear about his visions:

> I knew a man in Christ above fourteen years ago,
> (whether in the body, I cannot tell; or whether out of the
> body, I cannot tell: God knoweth;) such an one caught
> up to the third heaven. And I knew such a man (whether
> in the body or out of the body I cannot tell: God
> knoweth); how that he was caught up into Paradise, and
> heard unspeakable words, which it is not lawful for a
> man to utter. Of such an one will I glory ... (*II Corinthians*
> 12: 2-5).

Thus Paul did not know whether the man he met was 'in the body'
or 'out of the body'. He spoke 'unspeakable words' which were
not 'lawful to utter'. It would appear that both the source and the
subject matter of the revelation were doubtful. Yet Paul asked for a
blind faith in himself from his followers, and was angry with those
who followed the Apostles who had been with Jesus. Ironically he
accused them of changing his gospel:

> I marvel that ye are so soon removed from him that
> called you into the grace of Christ unto another gospel:
> which is not another; but there be some that trouble you,
> and would pervert the gospel of Christ. But though we,
> or an angel from the heaven, preach any other gospel
> unto you than that which we have preached unto you,
> let him be accursed. As we said before, so say I now again,
> if any man preach any other gospel unto you than that
> ye have received, let him be accursed. (*Galatians* 1: 6-9).

A little further on in the same epistle he mentions James, Peter and
Barnabas by name and says:

> I saw that they walked not uprightly according to the
> truth of the gospel. (*Galatians 2: 14*).

These verses clearly indicate the existence of 'another gospel'. There
is no record of the *Injil*, the revelation which Jesus received from
God, ever having been reduced to a written form exactly as it was
revealed. Paul was probably referring to the eye-witness accounts
of the life of Jesus, such as the *Gospel of Barnabas*, which were so
ruthlessly destroyed three centuries later after the Council of Nicea.

It is possible that Paul sincerely and ardently believed in his
actions. However, his misguided zeal was just as harmful in his
attempts to redirect the Nazarenes as when he had actively persecuted them: Paul's teaching had major consequences which he probably did not foresee, and which probably developed after his death.
His 'gospel of Christ' not only resulted in further changes being
made to what Jesus had taught, but also prepared the way to completely changing people's ideas of who Jesus was. The record of
Jesus the man was gradually being transformed into a conception
in people's minds. Jesus became a concept which was then capable
of manipulation. Paul's figure of Christ who apparently had the
power to annul what Jesus had previously taught, was clearly no
ordinary mortal, and inevitably became confused with God by
many. Thus this imaginary figure, separate from, yet linked by Paul
with Jesus, became an object of worship, and was often mistaken
for God. This led many to put Mary in the impossible position of
being regarded as the 'mother' of God.

This shift of emphasis from Jesus as a Prophet to the new image
of Christ who was Divine, enabled the intellectuals in Greece and
in Rome to assimilate what Paul and those who followed him were
preaching into their own philosophy. Their view of existence was
a tripartite one and with the Paulinians' talk of 'God the Father'
and 'the son of God' it only needed the instatement of the Holy
Ghost (in fact the angel Gabriel), to have a Trinity which matched
up with theirs. St. Augustine of Hippo, who lived from 354 to 430
AD, was not altogether happy with this, and envied the liberties of
the European philosophers:

> The philosophers speak their words freely ... We however do not say whether there are two or three principles, two or three gods. [5]

Plato's philosophy was based on a threefold distinction of the First Cause, the Reason, or *Logos*, and the Soul, or Spirit, of the Universe. Gibbon writes:

> His poetical imagination sometimes fixed and animated these metaphysical abstractions; the three archical or original principles were represented in the Platonic system as three gods, united with each other by a mysterious and ineffable generation; and the *Logos* was particularly considered under the more accessible character of the Son of an eternal Father, and the Creator and Governor of the world. [6]

With the passage of time and the arbitrary identification of 'Christ' with Plato's '*Logos*', the two pictures merged into one, and the doctrine of the Trinity was born, became established and finally was considered to be 'orthodox' Christianity:

> The pagans, who had then embraced the Gospel, and who were in some measure versed in the heathen philosophy, remarking this resemblance of terms, persuaded themselves that the Apostles believed the same things, in respect of these matters, as the Platonic Jews and pagans. And this seems to be that which drew several philosophers of this sect into the Christian religion, and gave such a great esteem to the primitive Christians, for Plato. [7]

Since everyone had different conceptions of what the Platonic terms meant, this led to even further schism amongst the Christians. Gibbon writes of the Christians of the second and third centuries:

> The respectable name of Plato was used by the orthodox and abused by the heretics, as the common support of truth and error. [8]

Paul himself never actually preached the divinity of Jesus nor the doctrine of the Trinity. His manner of expression and the changes he did make, however, when they were fused with the Platonic doctrines, opened the door to both these misconceptions, and prepared the way for their becoming the established doctrines of the Roman Catholic Church. What Paul had done to the teaching of Jesus, others did to his teaching. This process culminated in the Trinitarian doctrines of Athanasius, which were accepted as the official 'orthodox' Christianity during the Council of Nicea in 325 AD.

The Athanasian Creed, which is named after Athanasius but which was composed about a hundred years after the Nicene Creed was formulated, has been attributed to the Roman Catholics of the North African Church:

> The P. Quesnel started this opinion, which has been favourably received. But the three following truths, however surprising they may seem, are now universally acknowledged: Firstly, St. Athanasius is not the author of the creed, which is so frequently read in our churches. Secondly, it does not appear to have existed within a century after his death. Thirdly, it was originally composed in the Latin tongue, and, consequently, in the western provinces. Gennadius, Patriarch of Constantinople, was so much amazed by this extraordinary composition, that he frankly pronounced it to be the work of a drunken man. [9]

It is significant that none of the books in the *New Testament* mention the doctrine of the Trinity. The one verse (*I John 5: 7*) which asserts the unity of the three who bear witness in heaven has long been known to be a forgery, again the work of the Roman Catholics in North Africa. The forgery was made public by Sir Isaac Newton, who found that some of the oldest manuscripts had not been altered:

> Of all the manuscripts now extant, above fourscore in number, some of which are more than 1200 years old, the orthodox copies of the Vatican, of the Complutensian

editors of Robert Stephens, are become invisible; and the two manuscripts of Dublin and Berlin are unworthy to form an exception ... In the eleventh and twelfth centuries, the *Bibles* were corrected by Lanfranc, Archbishop of Canterbury, and by Nicholas, a cardinal and librarian of the Roman church, *secundum orthodoxam fidem*. Notwithstanding these corrections, the passage is still wanting in twenty-five Latin manuscripts, the oldest and the fairest; two qualities seldom united, except in manuscripts ... The three witnesses have been established in our Greek Testaments by the prudence of Erasmus; the honest bigotry of the Complutensian editors; the typographical fraud, or error, of Robert Stephens in the placing of a crotchet; and the deliberate falsehood, or strange misapprehension, of Theodore Beza. [10]

The inevitable extension and consequence of the doctrine of the Trinity was the doctrine of Incarnation, which was the bone of contention of the stormy Councils of Ephesus in 431 AD and of Chalcedon in 451 AD. For once it had been established that 'Jesus was God' by the Council of Nicea:

... the Catholics trembled on the edge of a precipice, where it was impossible to recede, dangerous to stand, dreadful to fall; and the manifold inconveniences of their creed were aggravated by the sublime character of their theology. They hesitated to pronounce that God Himself, the second person of an equal and consubstantial trinity, was manifested in the flesh; that a being who pervades the universe, had been confined in the womb of Mary; that His eternal duration had been marked by the days, and months, and years, of human existence; that the Almighty had been scourged and crucified; that His impassable essence had felt pain and anguish; that His omniscience was not exempt from ignorance; and that the source of life and immortality expired on Mount Calvary. These alarming consequences were affirmed with unblushing simplicity by Apollinaris, Bishop of Laodicea, and one of the luminaries of the church. [11]

The confusion in holding to the doctrine of Incarnation was only heightened by the mistaken belief that it was Jesus who had been crucified. It was not until the Council of Constantinople in 680 AD that the creed was finally settled, which teaches the Catholics of every age that two wills or energies were harmonised in the person of Christ. Thus Roman Catholicism as such was not established in Great Britain, writes Gibbon, until:

> ... the end of the seventh century, when the creed of the Incarnation, which had been defined at Rome and Constantinople, was uniformly preached in the remote islands of Britain and Ireland; the same ideas were entertained, or rather the same words were repeated, by all the Christians whose liturgy was performed in the Greek or the Latin tongue. [12]

It is not surprising, therefore, that there is no authentic mention of the doctrine of Incarnation in the *New Testament*. The one verse which states that God was manifested in the flesh is, again like *I John 5: 7*, a forgery:

> This strong expression might be justified by the language of St. Paul (*I Timothy 3: 16*), but we are deceived by our modern *Bibles*. The word '*o*' (which) was altered to '*theos*' (God) at Constantinople in the beginning of the sixth century: the true reading, which is visible in the Latin and Syriac version, still exists in the reasoning of the Greek, as well as of the Latin fathers; and this fraud, with that of the three witnesses of St. John, is admirably detected by Sir Isaac Newton. [13]

The doctrine of Incarnation is implied in the opening verses of John's gospel, but, as the length of time taken to formulate the doctrine indicates, these verses are as ambiguous as the doctrine itself. John's gospel, written about half a century after Paul's death, enshrines the Platonic philosophy. It was not written by John the Apostle and it is not an eye-witness account of Jesus's life and teachings. It is very different from the other three surviving synoptic gospels and sometimes contradicts them. However the Roman Catholic Church has claimed it to be the divinely inspired Word of

God, and as such free of all errors. Even this gospel contains no mention of the terms 'Trinity' or 'Incarnation', but the spurious authority it gives to the Platonic doctrine has been used to support the doctrines of Trinity and Incarnation – doctrines which Jesus, and even Paul, never preached.

○   ○   ○   ○   ○

What happened to the Nazarenes? They were comprised mainly of the followers of Jesus, peace be on him and them, many of them his apostles and closest disciples. They attracted many people to their number after he had disappeared. Two communities were formed, one in Jerusalem whose leader was James, and another in Antioch whose leader was Barnabas:

> To them what Jesus had taught was the Truth and the whole Truth. Barnabas and his followers continued to preach and practise the Christianity they had learned from Jesus himself. [14]

Following the example of Jesus, they continued to adhere to the fundamental practices of Moses which Jesus had retained: They affirmed the Divine Unity. They prayed in the synagogue at the appointed times. They fasted as Jesus had fasted. Each year they paid a tenth of their wealth into a common fund and then redistributed it amongst the poor in their community. They observed the Sabbath, the Passover, and the holy days. They practised circumcision. They killed the animals they were permitted to eat in the name of their Creator, and in the manner Moses and Jesus had indicated. The whole pattern of their behaviour was in accordance with that of these two Prophets, peace be on them. Armed with the strength of the Mosaic law, and by the illumination that Jesus had given them, they worshipped their Lord in the manner He had indicated:

> 'The first fifteen Bishops of Jerusalem,' writes Gibbon, 'were all circumcised Jews; and the congregation over which they presided united the law of Moses with the doctrine of Christ.' [15]

The Romans and the Gentiles made little or no distinction between the Nazarenes and the Jews. There was a general persecution of the Jews which culminated in the destruction of the temple of Solomon in 70 AD. Almost the entire Jewish population of Jerusalem was massacred, and many of the Nazarenes shared their fate. Those who escaped settled in Pella, a little town beyond the Jordan. When Hadrian later became emperor, in 117 AD, he founded a new city on Mount Sion. It was called Aelia Capitolina. Severe penalties were fixed for any Jew who even dared to approach it. Gibbon writes:

> The Nazarenes had only one way left to escape the common proscription ... They elected Marcus for their bishop, a prelate of the race of the Gentiles, and most probably a native either of Italy or of some of the Latin provinces. At his persuasion, the most considerable part of the congregation renounced the Mosaic law, in the practice of which they had persevered above a century. By this sacrifice of their habits and privileges, they purchased a free admission into the colony of Hadrian, and more firmly cemented their union with the Catholic Church. [16]

The Nazarenes who refused to make this compromise were condemned as heretics and schismatics. Some remained in Pella, some moved into the villages surrounding Damascus, and many of them settled in Aleppo in northern Syria:

> The name of Nazarenes was deemed too honourable for those Christian Jews, and they soon received, from the supposed poverty of their understanding as well as of their condition, the contemptuous epithet of Ebionites (the Poor). [17]

In Rome the pattern of persecution was the same. It was a group of people known as the Galileans, comprised of Nazarenes and Zealots, who were held responsible by Nero, and punished for, the great fire of Rome. The Nazarenes were also expected to pay the exacting taxes which were exclusively directed at the Jews in Rome:

> As a very numerous though declining party among the Christians still adhered to the law of Moses, their efforts to dissemble their Jewish origin were detected by the decisive test of circumcision. [18]

The persecution of the Nazarenes, and of all those who subsequently followed their example despite such persecution, bring the
following verses of John's Gospel to mind:

> They shall put you out of the synagogues: yea, the time
> cometh, that whosoever killeth you will think that he
> doeth God service. (*John 16: 2*).

The early persecution of the Nazarenes had a disruptive effect on
them, but it also spread them throughout the Roman Empire. Although their numbers were initially diminished, the teaching of
Jesus was made accessible to more people by their being scattered
over a wide area. To begin with there had been one or two communities, whereas now the seeds of many communities were sown. In
seeking to destroy the Nazarenes the persecutors had ensured their
survival:

> The communities they formed retained the life-style of
> Jesus. Although the time came when what these people
> knew by heart began to be recorded in writing, those
> who still embodied Jesus's teaching transmitted much
> of their knowledge directly from person to person. Be-
> haviour was imitated and the doctrine of Jesus passed
> on orally. They continued to affirm the Divine Unity. [19]

As the immediacy of Jesus's life began to recede, people began to
write down what they remembered or had learnt of his life and
teaching. It is likely that each small community, probably centred
round a particular disciple or apostle, had its own written record.
It is known that there were many such records:

> In time, many different written accounts of Jesus's life
> and teachings – some clearly more reliable than others
> – appeared and were used. Jesus had spoken in Ara-
> maic, a dialect of Arabic, which was not commonly writ-
> ten. The first Gospels were therefore usually recorded
> in Hebrew. In these early days, none were formally ac-
> cepted or rejected. It was up to the leader of each Chris-
> tian community to decide what books he would use.
> Depending on whom they had been taught by, each com-

munity or sect went to a different source. Those who followed Barnabas's example, for instance, went to one source – and those who followed Paul went to another.[20]

When the immediate followers of Jesus began to die out, their successors were chosen by all members of the community. These leaders were chosen on the criterion that they were the men who could best guide the community because of the extent of their knowledge and fear of God. As Gibbon points out:

> They could not possess, and would probably have rejected, the power and pomp which now encircles the tiara of the Roman pontiff, or the mitre of a German prelate.[21]

They were the servants of the servants of God. However with the passage of time this position often became the goal of those who wanted power. The presbyters and bishops, as the leaders came to be called, often became involved in politics, especially after the institution of the synods. The hierarchy of the priesthood, an institution entirely foreign to the teaching of Jesus, began to emerge.

The Romans did not view the emergence of the 'Early Church' very favourably. They attempted to uphold the worship of their gods. In the first three centuries after the disappearance of Jesus they probably did not always distinguish between the Nazarenes and the Paulinian Christians. The term 'Christian' was used to describe both those who followed Jesus and those who believed in Christ. If a man said he believed in God and refused to pay homage to the Roman gods, that was sufficient to establish his guilt. He was liable to imprisonment, confiscation of his goods, and often death. Gibbon remarks on the irregular conduct of their persecutors:

> … who contrary to every principle of judicial proceeding, admitted the use of torture in order to obtain, not a confession, but a denial, of the crime which was the object of their inquiry.[22]

The early persecution of the 'Christians' culminated in the edict passed by Diocletian and Galerius in 303 AD. It was the last and final attempt to abolish 'Christianity' in whatever form it had taken.

Churches were confiscated, gospels burnt, and all 'Christians' were placed outside the protection of the law. They could be prosecuted, but they were not allowed to defend themselves. When the edict was first nailed to the door of a church it was torn down by a Christian who was promptly but slowly roasted alive. The persecution was directed mainly at those who were recognisably followers of Jesus. For by this time the Paulinian Christians, not distinguishable by the outward observance of a guidance they refused to follow, were beginning to permeate the whole structure of the Empire:

> In the reign of Diocletian, the palace, the courts of justice, and even the army, concealed a multitude of Christians, who endeavoured to reconcile the interests of the present with those of a future life. [23]

Paul's religion, which had initially not been favourably received, became popular after the destruction of the Temple of Solomon and of Jerusalem in 70 AD, and after the savage repression of the *Bar Koch'eba* rebellion of the Jews in 132 AD. Paul's followers were not persecuted in the same ruthless manner which the followers of Moses and Jesus suffered. As has been seen, Paulinian Christianity was also found to be far more palatable to the people who were not Jewish by birth. In Gibbon's words:

> When numerous and opulent societies were established in the great cities of the empire, in Antioch, Alexandria, Ephesus, Corinth, and Rome, the reverence which Jerusalem had inspired to all the Christian colonies insensibly diminished ... The Nazarenes, who had laid the foundations of the church, soon found themselves overwhelmed by the increasing multitudes that from all the various religions of polytheism enlisted under the banner of Christ; and the Gentiles who, with the approbation of their peculiar apostle (Paul), had rejected the Mosaic ceremonies, at length refused to their more scrupulous brethren the same toleration which at first they had humbly solicited for their own practice. [24]

Thus quite soon after Jesus had left the earth there was a definite and widening divergence between the people who followed him and the people who followed Paul. Differences between the two were not only evident in life-style and belief, but were also delineated geographically. Whilst Paul's version of Christianity spread up through Greece and then Europe, the followers of Jesus and their followers spread with their knowledge to the East and to the South, and eventually right across North Africa. As we shall see in more detail further on, *insh'Allah*, their teachings also subsequently spread to the North and were eventually adopted by the Goths.

As the Pauline church became more established it grew increasingly hostile to the followers of Jesus. It became a matter of doubt and controversy whether a man who sincerely acknowledged Jesus as the Messiah, but who still continued to observe the law of Moses, could possibly hope for salvation. The Nazarenes and their successors, rejected by the Jews as apostates, were denounced as heretics by the Paulinian Christians. The Paulinian Christians thus separated themselves from the followers of both Moses and Jesus:

> They aligned themselves more and more with the rulers of the Roman Empire, and the persecution which to begin with had been directed at all who called themselves Christians, now began to fall mainly on those who affirmed the Divine Unity. [25]

The Paulinian Christians had compromised the guidance of Jesus to such an extent that they no longer posed a threat to the structure of authority into which they were being assimilated.

It is clear that generalisations such as 'the early Christians' and 'the early Church' are inadequate. They have traditionally been used to disguise the fact that there was once not one body, but two: a body of people called the Nazarenes who believed in Jesus and followed Jesus, as well as the body of people called the Christians who believed in Christ and followed Paul. The institution which arose out of Paul's teachings can be conveniently referred to as 'the Official Church', in order to distinguish this body from those who continued to follow the original teachings and example of Jesus, peace be upon him and them.

     o   o   o   o   o

Chapter Two

The Donatists
and the
Arians

When Constantine became Emperor, in 312 AD, he realised that it was impossible to eradicate Christianity, in whatever form, from the Roman Empire. Rather than let it divide the Empire he therefore attempted to use Christianity as a means of unifying it. He hoped to make the altars of the Official Church a convenient footstool to the throne of the Empire. As Gibbon makes clear:

> The throne of the emperors would be established on a fixed and permanent basis, if all their subjects embracing the Christian doctrine should learn to suffer and obey. [1]

Constantine therefore embarked on a policy of integrating the religion of the Official Church with the old Roman state religion. He did not publicly accept or reject either one of them in favour of the other. He patronised both. His actions seem to indicate that his toleration of the Official Church was based on political expediency and that he desired to maintain his position as emperor, and not to become a Christian. Constantine began his policy of integration by repealing all the laws of Galerius and Diocletian. In 313 AD he and Licinius, his brother-in-law who commanded the eastern half of the Empire, issued the edict of Milan:

> The two emperors proclaim to the world that they have granted a free and absolute power to the Christians, and to all others, of following the religion which each individual thinks proper to prefer, to which he has addicted his mind, and which he may deem the best adapted to his own use. [2]

Whilst tolerating the Official Church, Constantine continued to pat-
ronise his ancestral religion. He liberally restored and enriched the
temples of the Roman gods. He increased the council of Olympus
by the apotheosis of his father Constantius. The coins and medals
of the Empire were impressed with the figures and attributes of
Jupiter and Apollo, of Mars and Hercules. He was considered by
many of his subjects to be the representative if not the manifesta-
tion of the Roman sun-god on earth:

> The devotion of Constantine was more peculiarly di-
> rected to the genius of the Sun, the Apollo of Greek and
> Roman mythology; and he was pleased to be repre-
> sented with the symbols of the god of light and poetry
> ... The Sun was universally celebrated as the invincible
> guide and protector of Constantine. [3]

Constantine united the Sabbath of the Official Church with the day
of worship of the sun-god. Jesus had celebrated the Sabbath on
Saturday, but due to Constantine's persuasion it was moved for-
ward a day to Sunday. In 321 AD:

> He artfully balanced the hopes and fears of his subjects,
> by publishing in the same year two edicts: the first of
> which enjoined the solemn observance of Sunday, (Con-
> stantine styles the Lord's day *'dies solis'*, a name which
> could not offend the ears of his pagan subjects), and the
> second directed the regular consultation of *aruspices*
> (divination by inspecting the entrails of sacrificed ani-
> mals). [4]

Constantine took full advantage of the fact that the symbol adopted
by the Official Church, the cross, was the same as that of the Roman sun-god. This symbol signified something different to each of
his subjects, depending on whether they were pagan or 'Christian',
but it was acceptable to both of these parties:

> He eventually erected in the midst of Rome his own
> statue, bearing a cross in its right hand; with an inscrip-
> tion which referred to the victory of his arms, and the de-
> liverance of Rome, to the virtue of that salutary sign ...

The same symbol appeared on the arms of the soldiers of Constantine: the cross glittered on their helmets, was engraved on their shields, was interwoven into their banners ... But the principal standard which displayed the triumph of the cross was styled the *Labarum* ...

It is described as a long pike intersected by a transversal beam. The silken veil which hung down from the beam, was curiously enwrought with the images of the reigning monarch and his children. The summit of the pike supported a crown of gold, which enclosed the mysterious monogram, at once expressive of the figure of the cross, and the initial letters of the name of Christ. [5]

Thus the style of dress worn by the 'Crusaders' who came nine centuries later, and the symbol which adorns so many Christian altars today, have their origin in the political manoeuvres of a pagan emperor.

Constantine made full use of the Official Church in maintaining discipline in his army. The authority of the bishops was used to ratify the obligation of the military oath. Deserters faced the added threat of excommunication. The regular correspondence which connected the bishops of the most distant provinces enabled them to provide Constantine with useful intelligence work.

Constantine encouraged his subjects to become Christians, promising them not poverty, but wealth:

> The salvation of the common people was purchased at an easy rate, if it be true, that, in one year, 12,000 men were baptised at Rome, besides a proportionable number of women and children; and that a white garment, with twenty pieces of gold, had been promised by the emperor to every convert ... [6]

However, Constantine made sure that the Official Church remained entirely subservient to the Emperor:

> The irresistible power of the Roman emperors was displayed in the important, and dangerous change, of the national religion ... It was long since established, as a fundamental maxim of the Roman constitution, that every rank of citizens were alike subject to the laws, and

that the care of religion was the right as well as the duty
of the civil magistrate ... The emperors still continued
to exercise a supreme jurisdiction over the ecclesiastical
order. [7]

However Constantine ensured that its members were kept com-
fortable:

The whole body of the Catholic clergy, more numerous
perhaps than the legions, was exempted by the emperors from all service, private or public, all municipal offices, and all personal taxes and contributions, which
pressed on their fellow citizens with intolerable weight;
and the duties of their holy profession were accepted as
a full discharge of their obligations to the republic ...
Eight years after the Edict of Milan, Constantine granted
to all his subjects the free and universal permission of be-
queathing their fortunes to the Holy Catholic Church ...[8]

Constantine gave generous gifts to the leaders of the Official Church
and their communities. As they grew in number and popularity he
began to discourage the worship of the Roman gods until he finally proclaimed to the world:

... that neither his person nor his image should ever-
more be seen within the walls of an idolatrous temple;
while he distributed through the provinces a variety of
medals and pictures, which represented the emperor in
an humble and suppliant posture of Christian devotion. [9]

❂   ❂   ❂   ❂   ❂

Constantine's policy of adopting the religion of the Official Church
as the new state religion was not achieved without a struggle. He
may not have been aware of the distinction between the Nazarene
Church and the official Pauline Church when he commenced his
policy of integration. However the Nazarene Church's refusal to
co-operate with him soon made the difference apparent. He therefore attempted to unify the early Church by encouraging the
Nazarene Church to merge with the official Pauline Church. This
approach did not always meet with success.

❂   ❂   ❂   ❂   ❂

The different positions adopted by the two churches and Constantine's attitude towards them are clearly indicated by the events which took place in North Africa during Constantine's reign. Here the members of the Nazarene Church were firm. They refused to accept the validity of the Official Church whose centre was now Rome and not Jerusalem. The people of Carthage had a long history of war with Rome. That Rome should be regarded as the new holy centre was therefore repugnant to them, especially since the change had come about through political expediency and not by the command of God.

The Unitarian Christians in North Africa had persistently refused to worship the Roman gods and follow the Roman emperors. They had also refused to make the compromises which the Official Church had made. The conflict both with the Roman rulers and with the Official Church came to a head with the election of a Unitarian priest called Donatus. He was chosen as Bishop of Carthage in 313 AD, the same year as the Edict of Milan, and he soon had about three hundred bishops under him, including one bishop in Rome.

The leader of the Official Church in Rome tried to have Donatus replaced by one of his own bishops, named Cacealian:

> The prestige of Constantine was such that, in the conflict which ensued, both parties appealed to him. It appears that they thought that whoever won his support would have no further battles to fight. This attempt to win the patronage of Constantine brought with it a very important change in the history of Christianity. For the first time it had become possible for schism and unorthodoxy to become an offence punishable by secular law. This secular coat of armour stood at the disposal of whoever could prove himself to be 'orthodox', and could then be used against those who differed from this new standard of orthodoxy. [10]

Constantine supported the official bishop, Cacealian. He tried to persuade the Donatists to do likewise, but they refused. He issued a decree which condemned Donatus and drew their attention to 'the advantage of worshipping the Supreme Deity in the proper manner.' [11] Two tribunals met to decide the affair and give both parties a 'fair hearing'. However the members of the tribunals were all from the Official Church, and their decisions were predictably unacceptable to the Donatists. All attempts to unite the two Churches having failed, Constantine decided to persuade the Donatists by force. The Roman army was called into action in the name of Christ and the Pauline Church.

The Donatists could not believe that the Romans, who had persecuted them for so long, had suddenly become 'Christians' overnight. The pagan army began a fearful massacre of the Donatists. Bishops were murdered in their churches and dead bodies were thrown into the wells. The generous provisions of the Edict of Milan only applied to those who did as the Roman Emperor wished. The extensive literature of the Donatists was so systematically destroyed that very little of it survives today. In this way a pattern for the treatment of 'heretics', which was to be followed for centuries, including the present one, was set.

⊙   ⊙   ⊙   ⊙   ⊙

The same struggle between the Official Church and the Unitarian Christians also took place in Alexandria, an important centre of Christianity. The leader of the Unitarians was a Libyan priest called Arius. He followed the teaching of Jesus implicitly, and refused to accept the innovations introduced by Paul. He declared that Jesus's prophethood which raised him in degree above other men was solely due to the will of God, but that he was essentially as human as any other man created by God:

> If Jesus was in reality the 'son of God', he argued, then it followed that the father must have existed before the son. Therefore, there must have been a time when the son did not exist. Therefore, it followed that the son was a creature composed of an essence or being which had not always existed. Since God is in essence Eternal and Ever-Existent, Jesus could not be of the same essence as God ... Since Jesus was created by God, his being was finite and so he could not possess the attribute of Eternity. Only God is Eternal. Since Jesus was a creature, he was subject to change like all other rational creatures. Only God is unchanging. Thus, he asserted, it was clear that Jesus was not God. [12]

Arius's views were not welcomed by Alexander and Athanasius, the leaders of the Official Church in Alexandria. They did their best to defame Arius and his followers, who, in accordance with the established practice, were condemned as 'heretics'. The whole city was divided over this issue, and when Constantine heard that fighting had broken out in the streets, he was compelled to act.

Constantine's experience with the Donatists had shown him that the use of force to achieve 'religious unity' was not successful, since the 'conversion' thus achieved was not very reliable. He therefore tried to exert his influence in a more amicable manner and wrote a long letter to both Alexander and Arius, in which he stressed 'religious unity', but without any reference to using Jesus as a guide:

> If we cannot all think alike on all topics, we can at least all be united on great essentials. As regards the Divine Providence, let there be one faith and one understanding, one united opinion in reference to God.

The letter concludes:

> Restore me then my quiet days and untroubled nights that I may retain my joy, the gladness of peaceful life. Else I must groan and be defused wholly in tears, and no comfort of mind till I die. For while the people of God, my fellow servants, are thus torn asunder in unlawful and pernicious controversy, how can I be tranquil of mind? [13]

Constantine's letter had no effect, and he therefore called a meeting in 325 AD of all the bishops in order to decide the question once and for all. This gathering, which Constantine presided over, is known today as the Council of Nicaea. It resulted in the official acceptance of the doctrine of the Trinity as the 'true' doctrine of 'orthodox Christianity'. The Nicene Creed was composed and written down. It had the following anathema appended as a direct rejection of Arius's teaching:

> But as for those who say, 'There was when he was not', and, 'Before being born he was not', and that he came into existence out of nothing, or who assert that the Son of God is of a different hypostasis or substance, or is created, or is subject to alteration or change – these the Catholic Church anathematises. [14]

The Official Church had finally achieved the Emperor's public recognition and approval. Its religion was the state religion. The consequences of the Council were far-reaching. They were in complete contradiction of the sentiments expressed in the Edict of Milan, which Constantine had proclaimed twelve years earlier. The four gospels, none of them eye-witness accounts, which the Official Church had adopted as their official scriptures, were given official status. All other accounts of the life and teaching of Jesus, many of them eye-witness accounts written by the first Nazarenes, were banned. They were either destroyed or made *Apocrypha*, that is hidden from the general public. Up until the Council of Nicaea there were at least three hundred different gospels.

After the Council of Nicaea it became a capital offence to possess an unauthorised Gospel. As a result about one and a half million Unitarian Christians were killed in the years following the Council's decisions. The fact that no early manuscript of any gospel written before 325 AD exists today, indicates that even the four gospels accepted by the Official Church are not the ones which were originally written. Alterations, deletions, and additions have been made, and the originals destroyed to disguise this fact:

> The Gospels, scattered and spasmodic and late, are already celebrating the Christ of faith, and celebrating him for their own time, and with the assumption that the last days were about to begin. It follows, therefore, that any dramatisation of the life of Jesus which uses the narrative form of the *New Testament* is already in a mire of its own making if it tries to turn Christ back into the hidden Jesus. Every boast about 'authenticity' is a sign of confusion … [15]

The Council of Nicaea, instead of bridging the gulf between the Christian sects, widened it, and it resulted, writes Gibbon, in 'a spirit of discord and inconstancy, which, in the course of a few years, erected eighteen different models of religion.' [16] Such an outcome was inevitable, for the only way in which unity between them could have been achieved would have been by returning to the original teaching and example of Jesus, peace be on him.

o   o   o   o   o

The significance of the Council of Nicaea lies in the fact that the religion of the Official Church was now the officially accepted state religion, and anyone who now professed any other belief faced punishment from the forces of the Roman Emperor. Thus the Arians, as in the case of the Nazarenes, the Ebionites and the Donatists, were labelled as 'heretics'. Their affirmation of the Divine Unity led to their persecution. Arius himself was poisoned and died in Constantinople in 336 AD.

○   ○   ○   ○   ○

Ironically, Constantine died affirming the faith of the Unitarian Christians, having been baptised two years before his death in 337 AD by Eusebius of Nicomedia, an Arian bishop. His son and successor, Constantius, was also an Arian, and for a while the Arians in the Eastern half of the Roman Empire had breathing space.

In 360 AD Constantius called the famous Council of Rimini. It was attended by a much larger gathering than the Council of Nicaea, since it was composed of over four hundred bishops of Italy, Africa, Spain, Gaul, Britain and the Balkans. The majority of the bishops were from the Official Church. However, a creed drawn up by the Arian bishops which stated that the 'son' was not equal or consubstantial with the 'father', was agreed to by the assembly. It was on this occasion that, according to Jerome, the world was surprised to find itself Arian. This creed was ratified at the Council of Seleucia. However, when the bishops of the Official Church realised what they had done, they withdrew their support and reaffirmed the creed of the Council of Nicaea and the still emerging doctrine of the Trinity.

The Official Church continued to become more established, especially in Rome, and finally found unqualified imperial favour during the rule of Theodosius:

> If Constantine had the advantage of erecting the standard of the cross, the emulation of his successor assumed the merit of subduing the Arian 'heresy'. Theodosius was the first of the emperors baptised in the faith of the Trinity. Although he was born of a Christian family ... the practice of the age encouraged him to delay the ceremony of his initiation, till he was admonished of the danger of delay, by the serious illness which threatened his life, towards the end of the first year of his reign. [17]

On being baptised in 380 AD, Theodosius issued a solemn edict, which proclaimed his own faith, and prescribed the religion for his subjects:

> It is our pleasure that all the nations, which are governed by our clemency and moderation, should steadfastly adhere to the religion which was taught by St. Peter to the Romans; which faithful tradition has preserved, and which is now professed by the pontiff Damasus, and by Peter, bishop of Alexandria, a man of apostolic holiness. According to the discipline of the apostles, and the doctrine of the gospel, let us believe the sole deity of the Father, the Son, and the Holy Ghost; under an equal majesty, and a pious Trinity. We authorise the followers of this doctrine to assume the title of Catholic Christians; and as we judge, that all others are extravagant madmen, we brand them with the infamous name of heretics; and declare, that their conventicles shall no longer usurp the respectable appellation of churches. Besides the condemnation of Divine justice, they must expect to suffer the severe penalties, which our authority, guided by heavenly wisdom, shall think proper to inflict upon them. [18]

Shortly after this edict Theodosius called the famous Council of Constantinople in 381 AD. In the words of Gibbon:

> A hundred and fifty bishops proceeded without much difficulty or delay, to complete the theological system which had been established in the Council of Nicaea. The vehement disputes of the fourth century had been chiefly employed on the nature of the Son of God; and the various opinions, which were embraced concerning the Second, were extended and transferred, by a natural analogy, to a Third person of the Trinity ... A final and unanimous sentence was pronounced to ratify the equal Deity of the Holy Ghost. [19]

It had taken nearly four centuries for a doctrine which Jesus had never preached to be accepted in his name, and finally established as 'the truth'. God, like Roman Gaul, was now apparently divided into three parts!

◉   ◉   ◉   ◉   ◉

In the reign of Constantine, the Official Church, or the Roman Catholic Church as it was now known, had been clearly subservient to the Roman Emperor. In the reign of Theodosius it began to exert its influence *over* the Roman Emperor:

> The decrees of the Council of Constantinople had ascertained the 'true' standard of the faith; and the ecclesiastics, who governed the conscience of Theodosius, suggested the most effectual methods of persecution. In the space of fifteen years, he promulgated at least fifteen severe edicts against the 'heretics'; more especially against those who rejected the doctrine of the Trinity ... [20]

These edicts form the foundation, and are the origin of all the laws which the Roman Catholic Official Church subsequently promulgated in its attempts to eliminate all beliefs other than its own, especially affirmation of the Divine Unity.

The edicts which were expressed in the language of declamation and invective were far-reaching and strictly enforced. Any law which the 'heretics' might attempt to use as a defence was automatically considered invalid. The edicts were directed against the leaders, the places of worship, and the persons of the 'heretics' themselves:

Their leaders were refused the privileges and payments which were so liberally granted to the leaders of the Official Church. Instead they faced the heavy penalties of exile and confiscation of property for preaching and practising their faith. They also had to pay the impossible fine of ten pounds of gold. By eliminating the leaders it was hoped that their followers would be compelled by ignorance and hunger to return within the pale of the Roman Catholic Church.

The rigorous prohibition of the use of their places of worship was extended to every possible circumstance in which the 'heretics' might assemble to worship their Lord. Their gatherings, whether public or secret, by day or by night, in cities or in the country, were equally proscribed. The buildings and the land which they had used for worship were confiscated.

All the followers of the 'heretical' leaders were left to the mercy of the general public. The anathema of the Official Church was complemented by the condemnation of the supreme magistrate. Thus a man could commit any outrage against a 'heretic' with impunity from the law. They were thus ostracised from society and excluded from all but menial work. Since they were not permitted to make a will or receive any benefit from a dead person's will, they soon lost what little property they had.

All citizens of the Roman Empire were encouraged to participate in the elimination of the 'heretics', who were put to death if they persisted in their faith. A special group of people were organised to facilitate the execution of the edicts and to deal with accusations and complaints against the 'heretics':

> Every Roman might exercise the right of public accusation, but the office of the 'Inquisitor of the Faith', a name so deservedly abhorred, was first instituted under the reign of Theodosius. [21]

Thus the origins of all the 'Inquisitions' which were instigated by the Roman Catholic Church and which culminated in the notorious Spanish Inquisition are derived not from the teachings of Jesus, but from the dictates of a 'holy' Roman Emperor.

Some of the first people to die on account of the edicts of Theodosius lived in Spain. As we are about to see in more detail a little further on, *insh'Allah*, belief in the Divine Unity had spread to Spain through the Goths from the North of Europe and through travellers from the North of Africa. The Unitarian bishop of Avila was called Priscillian. In accordance with the edicts of Theodosius, he and six others were tortured, condemned and executed in 385 AD by the sentence of the Praetorian Prefect. Two bishops were also sent into exile to the Isles of Scilly. As was always the case in the persecution of 'heretics', Priscillian and his followers were accused of the most foul and degrading acts of self-gratification:

> But an accurate, or rather a candid, inquiry will discover that if the Priscillianists violated the laws of nature, it was not by the licentiousness, but by the austerity of their lives. They absolutely condemned the use of the

marriage-bed; and the peace of families was often disturbed by indiscreet separations. They enjoined, or recommended, a total abstinence from all animal food; and their continual prayers, fasts and vigils, inculcated a rule of strict and perfect devotion. [22]

The manner in which the trial of Priscillian took place was clumsy, in that the duplicity between the leaders of the Official Church and the officials of the Roman Empire was patently obvious. The Praetor had received an appeal and pronounced sentence in a matter of faith, while the bishops had exercised the function of accusers in a criminal prosecution. With the passage of time this duplicity was made more 'respectable':

> Since the death of Priscillian, the rude attempts of persecution have been refined and methodised in the Holy Office, which assigns their distinct parts to the ecclesiastical and secular powers. The devoted victim is regularly delivered by the priest to the magistrate, and by the magistrate to the executioner; and the inexorable sentence of the Church which declares the spiritual guilt of the offender, is expressed in the mild language of pity and intercession. [23]

○   ○   ○   ○   ○

It was during the reign of Theodosius that the Roman Catholic Official Church finally established its authority over the office of The Roman emperor. In using the religion of the Official Church to unify his empire, Constantine had ensured that its leaders remained subservient to him, and he had retained control over them. Once the hierarchy of the priesthood was established in the land, however, it began to exert more influence over the common people. The army, which the Emperors in the past had used to assert their authority, was now largely composed of 'Christians'. Their allegiance was now divided between the priests of the Official Church and the Emperor. In order to retain their popular support, the emperors after Constantine found it increasingly necessary to seek the support of the priesthood. As the priesthood grew aware of the power they wielded over the people, they were only prepared to support the Emperor if he did as they wished.

Thus in the reign of Theodosius, it was Ambrose, the Trinitarian Archbishop of Milan, who won the support of the common people. He exerted his influence over Theodosius to a degree which Constantine would never have countenanced or envisaged. The advisers of Theodosius were all followers of Ambrose, and even the Emperor's most secret counsels were immediately communicated to the archbishop. Since Theodosius too was a 'Christian', however, and under the illusion that he could only attain to God by the means and with the help of the priesthood, he felt compelled to accept this state of affairs.

The degree of Ambrose's influence over Theodosius is clear from their respective actions in the following incidents:

In the first incident, a Unitarian Christian church and a Jewish synagogue were burnt down in Callinicum, a small town in Persia, by some Trinitarian monks. They were told by the Roman magistrate to either rebuild these places of worship or else provide the money to do so. Theodosius ratified this decision. Ambrose told Theodosius that the magistrate's decision should be annulled, since the monks had only destroyed 'a mere synagogue, the haunt of infidels, the home of the impious, the hiding place of madmen, which was under the damnation of God Himself.' [24]

As this private warning did not produce an immediate effect, the archbishop publicly addressed the emperor from his pulpit, and refused to continue the service until he had obtained from Theodosius a solemn promise which secured the impunity of the bishop and the monks of Callinicum.

In the second incident, some of the inhabitants of Thessalonica murdered a Roman general. Acting under the orders of Theodosius, the inhabitants of the city were invited to the public games. Once they had gathered in the amphitheatre they were butchered by the Roman army. When Ambrose heard of this, he ordered the emperor to do penance. Theodosius accordingly refrained from going to communion for several months and mourned his action. Finally, he made his way to the church:

> He was stopped in the porch by the archbishop, who in the tone and language of an ambassador of heaven, declared to his sovereign that private contrition was not sufficient to atone for a public fault, or to appease the justice of the offended deity. [25]

Ambrose, who in accordance with one of the many new 'traditions' established by the Official Church, had assumed the power to absolve wrong actions – a power which in fact only belongs to God – demanded a rigorous penance from the Emperor. The usual penance fixed by the Roman Catholic Church for homicide was excommunication for twenty years. If this had been applied to Theodosius, who was responsible for the deaths of several hundred people, it would have been impossible to fulfil the penance before he died. Ambrose made a concession and reduced the period of excommunication to eight months, and, writes Gibbon:

> It was sufficient that the emperor of the Romans, stripped of the ensigns of royalty, should appear in a mournful and suppliant posture; and that, in the midst of the church of Milan, he should humbly solicit, with sighs and tears, the pardon of his sins. [26]

Such was the utility and efficacy of the innovation of 'confession'. It was a practice which both Jesus and his true disciples never followed, and a means of persuasion of which the Official Church made full use in order to exert its influence in the land.

    ❍   ❍   ❍   ❍   ❍

By the end of the reign of Theodosius, the Roman Catholic Official Church had all the resources of the Roman Empire at its command to establish its doctrines and to eliminate any other beliefs. It had grown so powerful that many people mistakenly equated the magnitude of its influence with the degree of its authenticity. Its origins had become lost in the past. It was now a long time since Jesus, peace be on him, had lived on earth. The history of the split between the Nazarenes and the followers of Paul had been conveniently covered over. Few people doubted the fallacious claims of power, wielded under 'divine authority', made by the Roman Catholic Church. Anyone who did, or who attempted to live as Jesus had lived and to affirm the Divine Unity as he had affirmed it, was removed by an institution which was now hand in glove with the rulers of the Roman Empire.

    ❍   ❍   ❍   ❍   ❍

With the passage of time the Roman Emperor became even more subservient to the Roman Catholic Church. The coronation of the Emperor became a strange religious ceremony, in which he was admitted into the lower orders of the priesthood and was made to anathematise all 'heresy' raising itself against the Holy Catholic Church. In handing him the ring, the Pope told him it was a symbol of his duty to destroy heresy; and in girding him with the sword, he was reminded that with this he was to strike down the enemies of the Official Church.

With the eventual collapse of the Roman Empire in the West, the Pope's influence became so great that it was he who now decided who should be the next Emperor of the 'Catholic Empire':

> The Vatican and Lateran were an arsenal and manufacture which, according to the occasion, have produced or concealed a various collection of false or genuine, of corrupt or suspicious acts, as they tended to promote the interest of the Roman Church. Before the end of the 8th century, some apostolical scribe, perhaps the notorious Isidore, composed the decretals and the donation of Constantine, the two magic pillars of the spiritual and temporal monarchy of the popes. This memorable donation was introduced to the world by an epistle of Hadrian I, who exhorts Charlemagne to imitate the liberality and revive the name of the great Constantine. [27]

By means of this forgery:

> The sovereignty of Rome no longer depended on the choice of a fickle people; and the successors of St. Peter and Constantine were invested with the purple and the prerogatives of the Caesars. So deep was the ignorance and credulity of the times, that the most absurd of fables was received, with equal reverence in Greece and in France, and is still enrolled among the decrees of the canon law. [28]

Thus the office of the Pope completely superseded that of the Roman Emperor. Once this transfer had been effected, the Pope was free to choose a 'Christian' figurehead who would retain the title of Roman Emperor, but remain the servant of the Official Church.

The Pope's choice of Charlemagne coincided with the ambition of Charlemagne himself, and when he was summoned to Rome he came eagerly:

> On the festival of Christmas, the last year of the eighth century, Charlemagne appeared in the Church of St. Peter; and, to gratify the vanity of Rome, he had exchanged the simple dress of his country for the habit of a patrician. After the celebration of the holy mysteries, Leo suddenly placed a precious crown on his head, and the dome resounded with the acclamations of the people: 'Long life and victory to Charles, the most pious Augustus, crowned by God the great and pacific emperor of the Romans!' The head and body of Charlemagne were consecrated by the royal unction: after the example of the Caesars he was saluted or adored by the Pontiff; his coronation-oath represents a promise to maintain the faith and privileges of the church; and the first fruits were paid in his rich offerings to the shrine of the apostle.' [29]

This trend of the increasing influence of the Church is evident from the contents of the Bull '*Unam Sanctum*' which was issued by Pope Boniface VIII several centuries later, on the 18th of November 1302 AD. It was the result of his confrontation with Philip IV of France. If it is compared with the edict of Theodosius, the reversal of roles performed by Roman Emperor and Official Church in the two documents is very marked. The Bull declared that there was one Holy Catholic Church, outside which there was neither salvation nor remission of sins. It asserted that the temporal sword and the spiritual sword were alike committed to the service of the Church. The spiritual sword was in the hands of the clergy, whilst the temporal sword was delegated to the secular authority on the understanding that it was to be wielded on behalf of the Church and under its direction. Since what was spiritual was greater than what was temporal, the temporal power was to be subject to the spiritual power, which was itself subject only to the judgment of God. Since, it claimed, relying both on *Mathew 16: 18-19* and on the forged decretals, the authority of the spiritual power had been divinely granted to St. Peter and his successors, it followed that to oppose it was to oppose the law of God Himself.

The forgery of the decretals, through which it is alleged that the spiritual monarchy of the world belongs to the Popes of the Roman Catholic Church, was not discovered until the sixteenth century AD. By this time the Official Trinitarian Church was so well established that even the discovery that its claims to authority were entirely fallacious could not shake the obedience of the minds it influenced. Similarly, it retained the land allegedly donated by Constantine, 'the fatal gift of Constantine' as Dante calls it, on which the Vatican was built and continued its business as usual. Thus Gibbon concludes:

> The popes themselves have indulged a smile at the credulity of the vulgar, but a false and obsolete title still sanctifies their reign; and, by the same fortune which has attended the decretals and the Sybylline oracles, the edifice has subsisted after the foundations have been undermined. [30]

This then is the story of how the Roman Catholic 'Official' Church originated and how its beliefs and policies first arose. Neither it, nor its principle doctrines were instituted or preached by the Prophet Jesus, peace be on him. Yet in the name of God and Jesus the Official Church reached a point where it not only considered itself able to define who a follower of Jesus was, but also felt itself obliged to eliminate all those who did not fall within this definition, especially those who affirmed the Divine Unity.

Chapter Three

The Visigoths

Despite the attempts of the Roman Catholic Church to crush Unitarian Christianity in North Africa and the Middle East, the chain of transmission of the original teaching from Jesus through his followers and their followers remained unbroken. It was by virtue of this transmission that belief in the Divine Unity was eventually embraced by the Goths. Through them it spread right across southern Europe, at the same time as the Official Church was becoming firmly established in Rome. The Goths have been much maligned because of this. The majority of historians have done their best to hide the fact that once the Goths became Arians their culture flourished as long as they held to the guidance which their Creator had given them. Instead they have usually been depicted as savage and unruly barbarians from their beginning to their end.

⊙   ⊙   ⊙   ⊙   ⊙

In spite of the diverse theories of their origin it appears now to be an accepted fact that the Goths originally came from the North of Europe, from the area which is today known as Poland. In about 280 BC they moved southwards from the area around the Baltic Sea and the mouth of the Vistula, looking for fertile land and a warmer climate. By 240 BC the Goths had settled in the south of Russia on both banks of the River Volga. From being shepherds they now became farmers. They formed into two distinct tribes. The Goths on the eastern bank became known as the Ostrogoths. Those on the western bank were called the Visigoths.

In the centuries which followed their numbers greatly increased. The Visigoths spread to the west and to the south. In the middle of the third century AD they made three great naval excursions to the south. In the third expedition they ravaged Nicaea and Nicomedia, destroyed the temple of Diana at Ephesus and sacked Athens. This coincided with the furious plague which, from 250 to 265 AD raged throughout every province, every city and almost every family of the Roman Empire.

In 269 AD the Visigoths moved *en masse* towards Italy. They were met and defeated by Claudius, who was surprised to find that the army had travelled with their entire families and possessions. It appears that they had intended to settle in Italy. There were further clashes between the Visigoths and the Romans during the rule of Auruleius, the successor of Claudius. However, both sides were considerably weakened by the recent fighting and the plague. A treaty beneficial to both of them was agreed on, intermarriage between the Goths and the Romans was encouraged, and peace was established. The most important condition of peace was understood rather than expressed in the treaty. Auruleius withdrew the Roman forces from Dacia, the area which roughly corresponds to modern day Romania, and tacitly relinquished that great province to the Goths and the Vandals, who were another of the great tribes of southern Europe at that time.

For fifty years there was peace. Then in 322 AD there was again fighting between the Romans and the Goths. Constantine outmanoeuvred them and another treaty was signed. This treaty was ratified ten years later in 332 by Constantine, that is, five years before his death, and at a time when he had begun to support Arius and his followers. A specified area of land was acknowledged as theirs, and they received an annual subsidy on the understanding that they would keep their peace with the Emperor.

+   +   +   +   +

It is not altogether clear whether or not the Goths came into contact with Unitarian Christianity before the appearance of the man called Ulfilas. Their encounters in Greece and near the borders of Italy must have provided them with some opportunity of doing so. However it is certain that it was during the lifetime of Ulfilas that Unitarian Christianity became firmly established amongst the Visigoths and Ostrogoths, both in their affirmation of the Divine Unity, and in the way they lived. It is because of this fact that the Official Christian historians have so derided and denounced not only the Goths but also all the other tribes of Europe who followed their example:

> The Ostrogoths, the Burgundians, the Suevi, and the Vandals, who had listened to the eloquence of the Latin clergy, preferred the more intelligible lessons of their domestic teachers; and Arianism was adopted as the

national faith of the warlike converts, who were seated
on the ruins of the Western Empire. This irreconcilable
difference of religion was a perpetual source of jealousy
and hatred; and the reproach of 'barbarian' was embit-
tered by the more odious epithet of 'heretic'. [1]

Ulfilas, a leader of the Visigoths, came to Constantinople shortly
after the death of Constantine, who was baptised in the last years
of his life by Eusebius of Nicomedia, and died in the Arian faith –
a fact which most official historians are eager to cover up, by stat-
ing simply that he became 'a Christian' towards the end of his life,
and trusting that most people will assume that by this they mean
that he became a Roman Catholic. Constantius, his son and successor, was also an Arian. Although Rome in the West had become the
centre of the Official Church, Constantinople in the East was at
this stage inhabited largely by Arians.

Whilst Ulfilas was in Constantinople, he met Eusebius of Nicomedia who was the supporter of Arius, the baptiser of Constantine, and the adviser of Constantius. Eusebius was one of the greatest leaders of the Arians. He taught Ulfilas all he knew. Ulfilas was
only thirty years old when, in 341 AD, Eusebius made him a bishop.
Ulfilas then returned to his people and it is not without reason that
the Emperor Constantius called him 'the Moses of our day'.

For the next forty years Ulfilas spread light amongst the Goths.
He brought a new way of life to them. He was the means by which
they experienced a new spiritual awakening. As a result, their culture flourished as it had never done before.

Although his teaching spread rapidly, Ulfilas inevitably met with
some opposition from amongst his own people, and especially from
those who preferred to worship the ancient gods and idols. The
majority of the Visigoths and Ostrogoths, however, embraced the
faith of Arius, and this new way of life eventually spread among
many of the other Teutonic tribes of Southern Europe, especially
during the rule of Hermanric, the king of the Ostrogoths, who by
370 AD had unified most of the different tribes of Europe, by conquering them all.

Up until this time, the tribes of Europe had relied entirely on an
oral tradition. Ulfilas invented an alphabet for the Gothic language
and then translated the *Septuagint*, namely the *Old Testament*, and
also one of the early gospels, from the Greek versions. From the
outset he was violently opposed by the Official Church whenever

he came into contact with its adherents. The fundamental reason for this was because he was a Unitarian. Furthermore, these translations of the Scriptures, which he made freely available to all of his followers, were not in keeping with the policy of the Roman Church. It discouraged any translation of the gospels into any language, and its own official gospels were only made accessible to the official priesthood. Since the gospel translated by Ulfilas was not one of the four officially approved gospels, he was hated all the more. A gulf, as wide as the one which had grown between the Nazarenes and the Paulinian Christians, existed between the followers of Ulfilas and the members of the Official Church.

During the following three centuries, the Official Church did its best to eliminate Arianism in the south of Europe in the same manner as it had dealt with the Donatists and the Arians in North Africa. As the subsequent history of the Arian Goths demonstrates, they did not reciprocate this behaviour when they were established as rulers in the land:

> Not withstanding these provocations, the Catholics of
> Gaul, Spain and Italy, enjoyed, under the reign of the
> Arians, the free and peaceful exercise of their religion. [2]

⊙   ⊙   ⊙   ⊙   ⊙

In about 375 AD, the first wave of marauding Huns who came from the East broke on the Goths. Ulfilas asked the Emperor Valens, who was also an Arian, if the Visigoths could enter the Eastern Roman Empire. The Emperor granted them permission to do so under certain conditions and promised them every help in settling down in their new home. One of the conditions imposed by the Emperor was that only Goths who were Arians were to be allowed to settle within the boundaries of the Eastern Empire. They were also told to surrender their arms. Ulfilas crossed the Danube at the head of about two hundred thousand Visigoths.

The officers who were sent to receive the Goths were corrupt and dishonest. They began to pick out the young women and boys to gratify their lust. They robbed the refugees of almost all that they possessed. Instead of seeing to their basic needs, the officers took advantage of them. They sold at a great price to the refugees first of all beef and mutton, and then, as supplies grew scarce, the flesh of dogs, diseased meat and filthy offal. When their money and possessions were exhausted, some Goths were driven to sell their wives and children. This picture of sensuality, greed and brutality is drawn not from Gothic sources, but from Roman historians. [3]

This tyranny continued through the winter of 376 and 377 AD, and still the Visigoths refused to break their promise to be peaceful citizens of the Empire. However, the time came when the patience of the Visigoths was exhausted. They attacked the small unit of the Roman army which was guarding them and easily overpowered them. They not only regained their women and children and possessions, but also all that the Romans possessed, including their arms.

After this initial success they began to roam the countryside in search of food without any let or hindrance. They helped themselves to whatever they could lay their hands on. Their movement soon took on the shape of a triumphal march, and they began to proceed towards Constantinople. When Valens heard of this he assembled his army and marched towards the approaching Visigoths. They met near Adrianople. Here a battle was fought in 378 AD. The Visigoths won a decisive victory and about two thirds of the Eastern Roman army was destroyed. Valens was wounded and died on the field of battle. He was succeeded by Theodosius, whose edicts were eventually the means by which the Arian Goths were eliminated. Thus, ironically, by killing an Arian emperor, the Visigoths helped to create the situation which ultimately led to their total destruction.

Theodosius did not openly attack such a large body of people, who had already decimated the Roman army in the East. He signed a treaty with them, and it was agreed that they should settle in Thrace. This they did, as if they were holding the land of their birth. Theodosius also promised an annual subsidy to them, provided they remained peaceful. Having concluded his treaty with the Goths, Theodosius marched to Constantinople where he summoned Damophilus, the leader of the Arians, and:

> ... offered that Arian prelate the hard alternative of subscribing to the Nicene creed, or of instantly resigning, to the 'orthodox' believers, the use and possession of the episcopal palace, the Cathedral of St. Sophia, and all the churches of Constantinople. [4]

Damophilus refused to do either and was immediately exiled.

Theodosius then arranged the election of Gregory of Nazianzus as the new Trinitarian bishop of Constantinople. He had to have an armed guard to protect him from the angry Arians in his triumphal procession through the streets of Constantinople:

> He beheld the innumerable multitude of either sex, and of every age, who crowded the streets, the windows and the roofs of the houses; he heard the tumultuous voice of rage, grief, astonishment and despair ... About six weeks afterward, Theodosius declared his resolution of expelling from all the churches of his dominions, the bishops and their clergy, who should obstinately refuse to believe, or at least to profess, the doctrine of the Council of Nicaea. His lieutenant Sapor was armed with the ample powers of a general law, a special commission, and a military force. [5]

Only the official version of what subsequently took place exists today. Suffice it to say that the Arian influence in Constantinople was destroyed. The Cathedral of St. Sophia was handed over to the Official Trinitarian Christians, and the Unitarian Arian places of worship were either closed or converted into Trinitarian Churches.

Once the Official Trinitarian Church was established in Constantinople, Theodosius began the business of establishing it wherever there were Arians. The rigour of his decrees, beginning with his edict of 380 AD, and their effects in the Western half of the Empire have already been discussed. Their consequences in the Eastern half of the Roman Empire were just as far-reaching.

It was inevitable that there should be a confrontation between Ulfilas and his followers on the one hand, and the combined forces of the Official Church and the Roman Emperor on the other. Many of the bishops in Constantinople who had professed to be followers of Arius soon declared themselves to be followers of Athanasius now that Theodosius was emperor. Their beliefs were founded more on political expediency and the desire for self-preservation than on conviction. If the Emperor of Constantinople was an Arian, then their synods would declare that Unitarian Christianity was orthodox Christianity. If the Emperor opted for Trinitarian Christianity, then the very same bishops would swiftly declare that it was the faith of the Emperor which was orthodox Christianity. As Gibbon points out:

> Religion was the pretence; but ambition was the genuine motive of episcopal warfare. [6]

Ulfilas was not a party to these politics. He had been made a bishop when the faith of Arius was accepted as orthodox Christianity, and when Athanasius had been denounced as a dangerous heretic. With the change on the imperial throne, Ulfilas refused to change his way of life, even though the followers of Athanasius were now in imperial favour. Despite the fact that many of the bishops who had supported Arius during the rule of Constantius and Valens had now renounced him, Ulfilas maintained the courage of his convictions. The beliefs and actions of Ulfilas and his followers were governed not by fear of the Roman emperor, but by fear of God.

Ulfilas challenged the doctrines of the Official Church with the boldness and conviction of Arius. The technical term which the Official Church had borrowed from Plato to establish the idea of consubstantiality within their doctrine of the Trinity, *'homousien'*, was condemned by Ulfilas as 'detestable and abominable'. He pointed out that it was nowhere mentioned in any of the gospels and declared that, 'it should be spurned and trampled on as an invention of the devil and the teaching of daemons.' [7]

For Ulfilas and his followers, their way of life was more than a mere outward profession of faith. In their eyes the form was as important as the belief. They knew that without the correct outward behaviour, their inward faith would mean nothing. Ulfilas and his followers never hesitated to affirm their faith in, and to worship, the One and only true God. He is, they said, Eternal, Incorruptible, Alone, Unbegotten, without beginning and without end. He cannot be associated with any form, and is by no stretch of the imagination a combination of parts. He is Single and Unchangeable.

Jesus, said Ulfilas and his followers, could not be equated with God. Jesus was not eternal. Jesus was a creature like any other man. Jesus could not create even a fly, whereas God is the Creator of everything. It was true that Jesus had been exalted among men by the design and will of God, but not by virtue of his essence.

Ulfilas and his followers also denied the 'divinity' of the Holy Spirit. Ulfilas described it as an illuminating and satisfying power neither God nor Lord but helper of Jesus, subject to him as Jesus is subject and obedient in all things to God.

When the Cathedral of St. Sophia and the churches of the Arians in Constantinople were forcibly taken over by the Official Church, Ulfilas declared that this was an act not of a Christian but of the Anti-Christ. The members of the Official Church, he said, were:

> ... not worshippers of God, but without God, not leaders but misleaders. [8]

He firmly believed that only those who followed the original teaching and example of Jesus could call themselves Christians. All other conventicles were not churches of God, but synagogues of Satan.

Ulfilas was undeterred by the harsh edict of Theodosius in 380 AD. He challenged the authenticity of the Official Church and the authority of Theodosius to pass such laws. He said that if they had any confidence in their faith and actions, they should be willing to meet him in a public disputation. Theodosius supported this idea, and in 381 AD he summoned Ulfilas and his followers to Constantinople. However on their arrival, Theodosius was persuaded by the Church to issue a decree cancelling the proposed council. The decree provided that neither privately at home, nor publicly, nor in any place whatsoever, should any disputation concerning the Christian faith be held.

Shortly after this Ulfilas mysteriously died while he was in Constantinople. The resemblance between the death of Ulfilas and that of Arius, who had died forty-five years earlier, is very marked. The death of Arius had been acclaimed as a miracle by the Trinitarian Church, but on closer examination had turned out to be a case of poisoning.

The following confession of faith was recorded at Ulfilas's deathbed:

> I, Ulfilas, Bishop and Confessor, have ever thus believed and in this the only true faith do I make this testament to my Lord. I believe that there is only one God the Father, Alone, Unbegotten and Invisible. [9]

In 1840 a manuscript written by Auxentius, Bishop of Milan and disciple of Ulfilas, was found. He describes Ulfilas as:

> A man who I am not competent to praise according to his merit, yet altogether keep silent I dare not. One to whom I, most of all men, am a debtor even as he bestows more labour upon me. For from my earliest years

he received me from my parents to be his disciple, taught me the sacred writings, manifested to me the truth, and through the tender mercy of God and the grace of Christ, brought me up both physically and spiritually as his son in the faith.

Ulfilas, he continues, 'was of most upright conversation ... a teacher of poetry and a preacher of truth.' [10]

○   ○   ○   ○   ○

Once Ulfilas was out of the way, Theodosius began the systematic conversion of the Visigoths. He commenced by calling the famous Council of Constantinople, to which reference has already been made, in 381 AD. It was this council which finally gave the Holy Ghost official status as the third member of the Official Christians' conception of the Trinity, and which ratified this doctrine as being 'orthodox' Christianity. Gibbon describes the bishops who 'belonged' to Theodosius and who came to this decision, which has so affected the world in the centuries which followed, in the following words:

> The sober evidence of history will not allow much weight to the personal authority of the fathers of Constantinople. In an age, when the ecclesiastics had scandalously degenerated from the model of apostolical purity, the most worthless and corrupt were always the most eager to frequent, and disturb, the episcopal assemblies. The conflict and fermentation of so many opposite interests and tempers inflamed the passions of the bishops: and their ruling passions were, the love of gold, and the love of dispute. Many of the same prelates, who now applauded the orthodox piety of Theodosius, had repeatedly changed with prudent flexibility, their creeds and opinions; and in the various revolutions of the church and state, the religion of their sovereign was the ruler of their obsequious faith ... The clamorous majority ... could be compared only to wasps or magpies, to a flight of cranes, or to a flock of geese. [11]

Gibbon adds that this picture comes not from any 'obstinate heretic', but from the Trinitarian bishop, Gregory of Nazianzus.

The official religion was soon established in Constantinople, and in the following years the decrees of Theodosius were relentlessly put into practice in the surrounding countryside. In 382 AD, only four years after the defeat and death of Valens, the general capitulation of the Visigoths in Thrace to the religion of Theodosius was well under way. Those who accepted Trinitarianism were allowed to stay. They were given an annual subsidy to keep them happy. Those Visigoths who resisted the decrees were pushed further and further northwards in the following years. In 395 AD, the same year as the death of Theodosius, they were finally expelled from Thrace.

During this time a systematic destruction of all the books written in the Gothic language was carried out. Virtually none remain today. After six centuries had passed the manuscript of a Gothic bible was found in the monastery of Werden near Cologne. It was written in the alphabet invented by Ulfilas. By the end of the sixteenth century the manuscript had found its way either by purchase or robbery to Prague. In 1648 it was removed from there and was presented to Queen Christins of Sweden. From Stockholm it passed into the hands of Isaac Vosseus. It was still in his hands when it was published in 1655 by Francis Jeuneus.

It was then discovered that of the original three hundred and eighteen pages in the manuscript, only one hundred and eighteen pages remained. One can only guess what happened to the missing two hundred pages. The remains of the manuscript are at present housed in the University of Upsala. The manuscript is inscribed in silver and gold letters upon a parchment of rich purple. The beauty of the craftsmanship and the importance of the text, which is written in a language which has otherwise perished, provide a solitary reminder of a people who once flourished and now are gone. It is regarded as one of the most important treasures of the world. In 1817 Cardinal Mai discovered some more pages of a gospel written in Gothic, but their contents have not been revealed.

⊙   ⊙   ⊙   ⊙   ⊙

The effects of Theodosius's persecution of the Visigoths not only rebounded on the Emperor but also helped to spread the faith of Arius further west. After the death of Theodosius in 395 AD, his successor Arcadius stopped the subsidy which was being paid to the Visigoths who remained in Thrace. This caused the Visigoths to unite, and with the emergence of their new leader Alaric (370-

410 AD), they revolted and formed an independent kingdom which extended from Thrace to Argos and from Athens to Sirmium.

Alaric moved west and down into Italy. In 401 AD he defeated the Roman Catholic army and conquered Rome. St. Augustine says that Rome did not suffer so severely in the days that followed its capture as it did under the eventual return of the Roman Catholic army. Far from following the conduct of the Official Christians, the Visigoths spared so many senators that it was only a matter of surprise that they slew some. Alaric gave orders that no building was to be burnt down, and the right of asylum was granted to all the Catholic churches. St. Augustine says that contrary to the usual customs of war this order was honourably observed. In all the scenes of terror and confusion, and despite all the opportunities of cruelty and rapine, lives were spared, women's honour was respected, and Catholic nuns were conducted by the Visigothic soldiers to a place of safety. [12]

After Alaric's death in 410 AD, his kingdom did not survive more than eighty years. Without a strong leader to unite them, the Visigoths gave way before the renewed attacks of the Roman Catholic army. However it was this very counter-attack by the Official Church which once again helped to establish the faith of Arius in another land: the Visigoths spread further west into Gaul and eventually into Spain. After the death of Wallia, Theodoric, son of Alaric, ruled western Gaul for thirty-two years, between 419 and 451 AD. He gave his two daughters in marriage to the kings of the Suevi and the Vandals, the two tribes who occupied Spain during his reign.

◗   ◗   ◗   ◗   ◗

It was towards the end of Theodoric's reign in Gaul that Attila the Hun commenced his famous invasion of Europe. It was said of Attila that the grass never grew on the spot where his horse had trod. The Huns led by him swept through Persia between 430 and 440 AD. They reached the borders of the Eastern Roman Empire in 441 AD. Their presence there and the threat of invasion caused the Romans to make generous treaties with Attila. The treaty of 446 AD included the payment of heavy taxes to the Huns in the form of food and wealth. These taxes were promptly paid by the Romans to appease the threatening hordes of Huns. When the embassy of Maximin came before Attila in 448 AD, they could only reply in the negative when he arrogantly asked:

> What fortress, what city, in the wide extent of the Ro-
> man Empire, can hope to exist, secure and impregna-
> ble, if it is our pleasure that it should be erased from the
> earth? [13]

The treaties made by the Romans, however, did secure the safety
of Constantinople and Rome. When Attila decided to move, he
marched from Hungary to Western Gaul in 451 AD. His forces,
already swelled by some of the Ostrogoths, were joined by those
of the Franks. Faced by a common enemy, Theodoric, son of Alaric,
combined with the forces of Italy who were led by Aetius, and they
marched on Attila who was besieging Orleans. Attila turned to meet
them, and the two armies clashed in the famous battle of Chalons.
Both sides lost many men. It is said that between 162,000 and 300,000
men were killed. Theodoric, son of Alaric, was killed in the battle
and his son Torismund became king of the western Visigoths.

The survivors of the battle withdrew. Aetius returned to Italy,
while Attila re-grouped his forces. In 452 AD he invaded Italy. He
reduced Aquileia to dust and captured Milan. The Italian refugees
fled to the empty area of little islands and waterways on the north-
eastern coast of Italy, where they began to build what is now the
remains of Venice. Attila was persuaded not to attack Rome. He
was given Honoria, a Roman princess, as a wife. He died on the
night of his wedding, due to excessive drinking, in 453 AD:

> An artery had suddenly burst; and as Attila lay in a su-
> pine posture, he was suffocated by a torrent of blood,
> which instead of finding a passage through the nostrils,
> regurgitated into the lungs and stomach. [14]

The timely death of Attila left Italy in even greater confusion, and
allowed the Arian Visigoths in western Gaul to continue their expansion unmolested. Torismund was succeeded by another king
called Theodoric, and he ruled in Toulouse from 453 to 466 AD. He
kept to the teachings which Ulfilas had first spread among the
Visigoths. His first church service was before daybreak. He ate with
temperance. During his reign the first incursion of the Visigoths
into Spain was made.

o   o   o   o   o

The state of Spain prior to the arrival of the Visigoths is all the more interesting, since it closely resembled the situation which existed prior to the arrival of the Muslims there some three centuries later: In the fourth century AD Spain was burdened with a corrupt and decaying feudal system. The Official Church had some influence there, having been established to some degree by virtue of the edicts of Theodosius. However, many of the Roman officials who governed the country would have nothing to do with this institution, preferring their own idols. Possession of the land was in the hands of the Roman aristocracy. These lords possessed large estates, lived for pleasure, and tyrannised the multitude of impoverished citizens who were their serfs and slaves:

> 'Once upon a time,' writes Seneca, 'it was proposed in the Senate that slaves should wear a distinctive dress. The motion however could not be carried for fear that our slaves might take to counting us.' [15]

The administrative work in this society was performed by the middle class, known as the burgesses. The Roman taxes fell mainly on them. The point was reached where they no longer considered their function profitable. Many of them fled into the forests, and with other serfs and slaves they formed marauding robber bands. These bands grew so large that in the reign of Diocletian, the Caesar had to undertake a large military operation against them. By the time of the reign of Constantine (312-337 AD), the north of Spain was rotten with debauchery and lawlessness.

When the Vandals and the Suevi swept down into Spain at the end of the fourth and the beginning of the fifth centuries AD, they met with no organised resistance from the Roman forces there. Both tribes had come into contact with the teachings of Ulfilas, but the Vandals were far more closely related to the Visigoths, and had embraced Unitarian Christianity as a result. The Suevi were far more warlike, and it appears from their subsequent behaviour in Spain that they preferred their idols.

The Vandals did not remain in Spain for very long, but passed through it and over to North Africa where, as we are about to see in more detail a little further on, *insh'Allah*, they united with the remaining Donatists and Arians who had survived the persecution of Theodosius. Through them Unitarianism was established in North Africa once more. The wheel had come the full circle.

The Suevi remained in Spain. The numerous robber bands joined them and increased their strength. They plundered at will, and many people were forced to seek refuge in the Visigothic kingdom in the south of France. A contemporary writer described the conditions in Spain at this time as follows:

> The poor are pillaged, the widows mourn, the orphans are trampled underfoot, so much so that many of them flee to the enemy seeking I suppose Roman humanity amongst the 'barbarians', when they could no longer bear the barbarous inhumanity among the Romans. So in spite of the difference of worship and habits they pass over to the Goths. [16]

This condition of social chaos in Spain lasted until the Visigoths arrived. They crossed the Pyrenees and defeated the army of the Suevi in a bloody battle on the banks of the Orvigo in 456 AD. Theodoric, king of the Visigoths in Gaul, then marched to Braga, the capital of the Suevis. There was hardly any fighting and the chastity of the women was respected. Most of the people were taken as slaves, however, and inevitably there was a good deal of plundering. Keeping to the west of the Iberian peninsula, the army of the Visigoths went as far as Merida before returning to Toulouse, where the peaceful rule of the Visigoths continued for another fifty years, until the sudden invasion of the Trinitarian Christian Clovis, King of the Franks, in 507 AD.

Towards the end of Theodoric's reign the Visigoths again moved south into Spain. Between 462 and 472 AD many of them settled there. In the years that followed the Visigoths spread further into the heart of Spain, bringing their way of life with them. Dozy writes that they, 'believed all that their priests taught them,' and that, 'they were naturally religious':

> In danger, they looked for help from God alone. Before a battle their kings prayed in sack-cloth, an act at which a Roman general would have scoffed; and if they were victorious they recognised the hand of the Eternal in their triumph. Further, they honoured their clergy, and not merely their own Arian clergy but the Catholic priesthood as well. [17]

o   o   o   o   o

Chapter Four

The Vandals

It is necessary at this point to examine the continued persecution of the Donatists in North Africa and to discover in more detail how the Arian Vandals of Northern Europe came down through Spain, united with the Donatists and ruled North Africa virtually up until the spread of Islam to North Africa.

❂   ❂   ❂   ❂   ❂

The persecution of the Donatists, which was commenced by Constantine, was continued by Theodosius and Honorius. The fifth title of the sixteenth book of the Theodosian Code exhibits a series of the imperial laws against the Donatists from the year 400 to the year 428 AD. Of these the fifty-fourth law, promulgated by Honorius in 414 AD, is the most severe and effectual. [1]

The persecution was both thorough and rigorous. Many of the Donatists preferred to die affirming the Divine Unity than to live in constriction and enforced silence. The principal targets of the persecutors were the leaders of the Donatists. Three hundred bishops and many thousands of lesser clergy were removed from their communities, stripped of their possessions and banished to various islands. If they attempted to return to Africa the penalty was death. Their numerous congregations, both in the cities and in the country, were deprived of their rights as citizens and were forbidden to worship God in their accustomed manner. A regular scale of fines, from ten to two hundred pounds of silver, was imposed on all who dared to attend a gathering of Unitarian Christian worshippers. After a person had been fined five times his future punishment was referred to the discretion of the imperial court.

By these measures, which were warmly approved of by St. Augustine of Hippo, great numbers of Donatists were forced to profess, at least outwardly, the religion of the Official Roman Catholic Church. Many, however, chose to fight to the last, and the country was filled with tumult and bloodshed.

Whilst this persecution was at its height in North Africa, the Vandals, who were Arians, and the Suevi, swept down into northern Spain. As we have already seen in the last chapter, the Suevi remained in the north of Spain, while the Vandals, under the leadership of Genseric, continued to move south. They defeated the Roman army in a decisive battle in mid-Spain:

> Salvian ascribes the victory of the Vandals to their superior piety. They fasted, they prayed, they carried a Bible in the front of the host, with the design, perhaps, of reproaching the perfidy and sacrilege of their enemies. [2]

In 428 AD Genseric conquered Seville and Cartagena, and the eyes of the Vandals gazed over the Straits of Gibraltar to Africa which, despite the unrest, was at that time very prosperous. The long and narrow tract of the North African coast was filled with Roman developments and monuments. It was very fertile and well cultivated. Although the large population retained a liberal proportion of the crops for themselves, the annual exportation, particularly of wheat, was so regular and plentiful that North Africa deserved the name of the common granary of Rome and of mankind.

Genseric considered settling there, and on receiving offers of help from the Roman general Boniface, who governed North Africa and who had recently accepted the faith of the Donatists, he resolved to do so. He was just about to make the crossing when he was informed that Hermanric, the king of the Suevi, had attacked and ravaged the territories which he was just about to abandon. Genseric turned about, drove the Suevi back as far as Merida and into the River Anas, and then calmly returned to the southern seashore of Spain, to embark his victorious troops. Genseric crossed over to Africa with all the Vandals and commenced his conquest of North Africa. He was welcomed by the Donatists:

> Genseric, a Christian, but an enemy of the orthodox communion, showed himself to the Donatists as a powerful deliverer, from whom they might reasonably expect the repeal of the odious and oppressive edicts of the Roman emperors. [3]

Thus a century after the persecution of Arius and Donatus was first initiated by Constantine, their followers met and recognised each other, after their respective teachings, the same teaching, had circulated right across Europe on the one hand and right across North Africa on the other. The North African Donatists merged with the Arian Vandals and, writes Gibbon, 'they enjoyed an obscure peace of one hundred years at the end of which we may again trace them by the light of the imperial persecutions.' [4]

The progress of the Vandals across North Africa was swift. Most official histories describe their conquest as bloody and tyrannical but, writes Gibbon, this destructive rage has perhaps been exaggerated by popular animosity, religious zeal and extravagant declamation. War, in its fairest form, involves hardship and pain. Plundering was inevitable, and where the Vandals found resistance, they seldom gave quarter. However, it is unlikely, as the official historians claim, that the Vandals destroyed the cities they intended to settle, and uprooted the olives and other fruit-trees on which they depended as a source of food. And it is hardly credible that it was a usual stratagem to slaughter great numbers of their prisoners before the walls of a besieged city for the sole purpose of infecting the air and producing a pestilence, of which they themselves would have been the first victims.

The Vandals reached Hippo, which is two hundred miles west of Carthage, a few months after St. Augustine had died there. His extensive writings were not destroyed by them, despite the fact that he had always supported the persecution of the Arians and the Donatists, and was himself a Trinitarian.

It is interesting to note in passing that St. Augustine had no knowledge of Greek or Hebrew which, many people say, barred him from any true study of the gospels:

> According to the judgment of the most impartial critics, the superficial learning of Augustine was confined to the Latin language; and his style, though sometimes animated by the eloquence of passion, is usually clouded by false and affected rhetoric. But he possessed a strong, capacious and argumentative mind; he boldly sounded the dark abyss of grace, predestination, free-will, and original sin; and the rigid system of Christianity, which he framed, or restored, has been entertained with public applause, and secret reluctance, by the Latin church. [5]

Genseric and the Vandals reached Carthage – which once stood near the site where the city of Tunis now stands – in 439 AD. From there he ruled both North Africa and the Mediterranean. He even attacked Rome, in 455 AD. It is said that he promised to harm no one and to respect people whatever their religion. However, his soldiers sacked and looted Rome for fourteen days before returning to Carthage. They left with many prisoners and all the treasures of Rome, including, it is said, the spoils which had originally been taken from the Temple of Solomon in the sack of Jerusalem by the Romans in 70 AD. However it appears that the allegations of needless damage done to the city are unwarranted or at least exaggerated. The *Encyclopaedia Britannica* is of the opinion that there does not seem to be any justification for the charge of wilful and objectless destruction of public buildings, which is implied nowadays in the word 'vandalism'.

Genseric's rule was long and fierce, and he did not grant the Roman Catholics the usual freedom to practise their religion which was typical of the vast majority of Arian monarchs. However he did nothing more than what the Roman Catholic Official Church had done when it was established in the land. He simply gave them a taste of their own medicine. There had been continuous persecution of the Donatists during the century prior to the arrival of the Vandals, and under such circumstances it is understandable that retaliation was almost inevitable. The most enlightened leaders of the Donatists, who would have been more prone to forgive and do as they would be done by, were long dead. The less discerning who now remained were understandably motivated by a desire for revenge.

During the early conquest of Africa by the Vandals, the Arian Visigoths in Europe remained aloof from Genseric's activities. When the Visigoths moved down into Spain during the second half of the fifth century AD, however, the Vandals in North Africa made an alliance with them. This is not surprising, since, as we have already seen, at this time the majority of both of these tribes were Unitarian Christians. Some Visigoths eventually crossed the straits and settled in the areas of North Africa nearest Spain. However on the whole these two tribes did not mix, although peace was kept between them.

In 477 AD Hunneric, the son of Genseric, became king. He continued to oppose the Roman Catholic Church with violence, although it is not clear how violent he was, for only the 'official' histories written by his enemies survive today, and they are clearly exaggerated. They hold the view that to kill a Unitarian Christian – whom they term a 'heretic' – who is actively following a Prophet of God is a necessary virtue, whilst any act of retaliation or self-defence by such a Unitarian Christian is regarded as an atrocious act of barbarism.

It would appear that Hunneric attempted to make peace with the Roman Emperor by saying that if the Unitarian Christians throughout the Roman Empire were given the same toleration and freedom of conscience as the Trinitarian Christians then he in turn would allow the Roman Catholics in North Africa to practise their religion freely. When this attempt at reconciliation failed, however, he then imposed all the laws, by which the Official Church had persecuted the Arians and the Donatists, on the Official Christians themselves. Those who had formulated and enforced the laws of persecution were now subjected to them:

> In the original law which is still extant, Hunneric expressly declares, and the declaration appears to be correct, that he had faithfully transcribed the regulations and penalties of the imperial edicts, against the heretical congregations, the clergy, and the people, who dissented from the established religion. If the rights of conscience had been understood, the Catholics must have condemned their past conduct, or acquiesced in their actual sufferings. But they still persisted to refuse the indulgence which they claimed. While they trembled under the lash of persecution, they praised the laudable severity of Hunneric himself, who burnt or banished great numbers of Manichaeans; and they rejected with horror, the ignominious compromise, that the disciples of Arius, and of Athanasius, should enjoy a reciprocal and similar toleration in the territories of the Romans, and in those of the Vandals. [6]

Hunneric used exactly the same tactics which the Official Roman Catholic Church had so often employed against the Arians and the Donatists. The practice of a conference, which the Catholics had so frequently used to insult and punish the Unitarian Christians, was used against themselves. At the command of Hunneric, four hundred and sixty-six orthodox bishops assembled at Carthage. When they were admitted into the hall of audience, they were dismayed to find that an Arian bishop was to preside over the council. There was a general uproar. Once the tumult had quietened down, the orthodox bishops were given the choice of accepting Unitarian Christianity or facing the penalties which the Official Roman Catholic Church had originally fixed for those who differed from the established religion.

As a result one martyr and one confessor were selected from among the Catholic bishops; twenty-eight escaped by flight, and eighty-eight by conformity; forty-six were sent to Corsica to cut timber for the royal navy; and three hundred and two were banished to different parts of Africa after being deprived of all their possessions.

The laws of persecution were imposed on all who rejected Unitarian Christianity. The Vandals adopted the practice of enforcing their form of baptism on the Trinitarian Christians. Anyone who refused to undergo this baptism, which scandalously violated their freedom of choice, was punished in accordance with the laws of the Official Roman Catholic Church, and the tortures which the Official Christians had used on the Arians and the Donatists were now inflicted on themselves.

Through the veil of fiction and declamation which pervades the official histories, it is evident that the Roman Catholics, more especially under the reign of Hunneric, endured the most cruel and ignominious treatment. Those who refused to worship in the Unitarian Christian churches were threatened with exile or death, and Gibbon dramatically describes at least one example of the mass expulsion of a large number of Roman Catholics from the land which the Vandals had settled:

> A venerable train of bishops, presbyters, and deacons, with a faithful crowd of four thousand and ninety-six persons, whose guilt is not precisely ascertained, were torn from their native homes by the command of Hunneric ... These unhappy exiles, when they reached the Moorish huts, might excite the compassion of a people, whose native humanity was neither improved by reason, nor corrupted by fanaticism: but if they escaped the dangers, they were condemned to share the distress of a savage life. [7]

Such actions, although an imitation of the methods of the Catholic Church, were outside the teachings of Arius and Donatus. No one benefited from them, and they only led to fierce retaliation by the Trinitarian Christians when the reconquest of Carthage by the Roman general Belisarius, in 533 AD, established the Official Church in Africa once more.

○　　○　　○　　○　　○

It is significant that many of the more famous forgeries perpetrated by the Official Trinitarian Church were made during this extended period of persecution by the Vandals in North Africa. The majority of the Vandals did not speak Latin, the language of the Official Roman Catholic Church, and therefore alterations to the text of the Latin bibles could be made with relative impunity. However those who were aware that further changes were being made to an already distorted message must have felt that their persecution of the Trinitarian Christians was justified under the circumstances, and that the measures taken by them were made in an attempt to protect and maintain the purity of what remained of Jesus's teaching.

Despite this, the Christianity of today owes much of its plausibility to the forgeries executed by the Official Christians of this period. These include, as we have already noted in Chapter One, the compilation of the Athanasian Creed and the invention of *I John 5: 7*. Gibbon writes:

> The orthodox theologians were tempted, by the assurance of impunity, to compose fictions, which must be stigmatised with the epithets of fraud and forgery. They ascribed their own polemical works to the most venerable names of Christian antiquity; the characters of Athanasius and Augustine were awkwardly personated by Vigilius and his disciples; and the famous creed which so clearly expounds the mysteries of the Trinity and the Incarnation, is deduced, with strong probability, from this African School. Even the Scriptures themselves were profaned by their rash and sacrilegious hands. The memorable text, which asserts the unity of the *three* who bear witness in heaven, is condemned by the universal silence of the orthodox fathers, ancient versions, and authentic manuscripts. It was first alleged by the Catho-

lic bishops whom Hunneric summoned to the conference of Carthage. (Or, more properly, by the four bishops who composed and published the profession of faith
in the name of their brethren. They style this text, '*luce
clarius*'. It is quoted soon afterward by the African po-
lemics, Virgilius and Fulgentius.) An allegorical inter-
pretation in the form, perhaps, of a marginal note, invaded the text of the Latin Bibles, which were renewed
and corrected in a dark period of ten centuries. After
the invention of printing, the editors of the Greek Testament yielded to their own prejudices, or to those of the
times; and the pious fraud, which was embraced with
equal zeal at Rome and at Geneva, has been infinitely
multiplied in every country and every language of modern Europe. [8]

Gibbon concludes by saying:

The example of fraud must excite suspicion: and the
specious miracles by which the African Catholics have
defended the truth and justice of their cause, may be
ascribed, with more reason, to their own industry, than
to the visible protection of Heaven. [9]

o   o   o   o   o

Hunneric was succeeded by Hilderic who became king in 523 AD.
He renewed the customary toleration of the Arians towards the
Roman Catholics. He issued an edict which restored two hundred
official bishops to their churches, and allowed free profession of
the Athanasian Creed. But the Catholics accepted with cold and
transient gratitude a favour so inadequate to their pretensions, and
Hilderic's tolerance was also criticised by the Vandals themselves.
Some of their leaders insinuated that he had renounced their faith,
and the soldiers more loudly complained that he had degenerated
from the courage of his ancestors.

Hilderic's tolerance was his undoing. The Roman Catholics, who
were not content to live in peace because they wanted power, plot-
ted his downfall. The army, supported by the Roman Catholics,
revolted and a general named Gelimer seized power. He was eventually defeated by Belisarius in 533 AD.

Belisarius had sailed from Constantinople under the orders of the Emperor Justinian. He disembarked his army at Tunis, and they then marched towards Carthage. It is said that he exhorted his army not to pillage and plunder, but to act humanely towards anyone who did not resist them. After a few days' march they met and defeated the Vandals outside Carthage. His victory was announced to the city on the eve of St. Cyprian, when the churches were already adorned and illuminated for the festival of the martyr, whom three centuries of superstition had almost raised to a local deity. The Arians, conscious that their reign had expired, released their church to the Catholics who performed their rites, and loudly proclaimed the creed of Athanasius and Justinian.

It was inevitable, especially after the acts of retaliation committed by the Vandals, that the persecution of the Arians and the Donatists should be recommenced by the Official Church, and once Belisarius had returned to Constantinople with Gelimer as his prisoner, this task was taken up in earnest. Indeed the reign of Justinian has been noted for its extensive persecution of those who refused to subscribe to the official religion:

> The reign of Justinian was a uniform yet various scene of persecution; and he appears to have surpassed his indolent predecessors, both in the contrivance of his laws and the rigour of their execution. The insufficient term of three months was assigned for the conversion or exile of all 'heretics'. [10]

(As we shall see in *Islam in Andalus, insh'Allah,* this ultimatum was exactly the same as the ultimatum which was given firstly to the Jews, and then to the Muslims, in the fourteenth and fifteenth centuries, prior to their mass expulsions from the Iberian peninsula.)

At the end of the three month term, all those who had refused to become Trinitarian Christians, but who had remained were killed. A bishop of the Official Church was given the title of 'Inquisitor of the Faith', the title first used by Theodosius and later adopted by the Mediaeval and Spanish inquisitions. It was his job to see that the elimination of 'heretics' was carried out efficiently and in a coordinated manner. Not only the Unitarian Christians but also the Jews, the Samaritans and all the variegated minor Christian sects, especially in the eastern half of the Roman Empire, suffered under this fresh wave of persecution and thousands were slaughtered:

> In the creed of Justinian, the guilt of murder could not
> be applied to the slaughter of 'unbelievers'; and he pi-
> ously laboured to establish with fire and sword the unity
> of the Christian faith. [11]

This extensive persecution again reduced the number of Unitarian
Christians in North Africa. The general population was further decimated by the plague which started by the Nile in 542 AD. It spread
to the East through Syria, Persia and the Indies, and to the West
right across North Africa and into Europe. Despite all this, affirmation and worship of the Divine Unity was continued in North
Africa by the followers of Arius and Donatus, until the coming of
Islam:

> When Islam came to them, they embraced it, so well-
> prepared were they for what was, after all, an extension
> and re-affirmation of the guidance they had been fol-
> lowing. [12]

○   ○   ○   ○   ○

Chapter Five

The Ostrogoths

Having briefly considered the early history of the Visigoths and the Vandals, it is now necessary to return to the early history of the other main tribe of the Goths, the Ostrogoths.

⊙   ⊙   ⊙   ⊙   ⊙

When the Visigoths spread West after the death of Alaric in 410 AD, the Ostrogoths followed in their footsteps and eventually descended into Italy. Their leader was a man called Theodoric, son of Theodomir, who lived from 454 to 526 AD.

As a child Theodoric was possessed of unusual beauty with striking long yellow hair. When he was seven years old he was sent as a hostage to Constantinople. Here the handsome noble-spirited boy soon endeared himself to the Emperor Leo. He stayed in the imperial palace for ten years. When he was seventeen, the Emperor returned him to his father with rich presents and good will. Scarcely had he returned home than the Roman governor of Bulgaria revolted against the Emperor. Theodoric immediately collected an army of 10,000 men and attacked Belgrade. He defeated the rebellious governor before the Roman Emperor had time to send the imperial army to crush the revolt.

In 474 AD, when Theodoric was twenty years old, King Theodomir died, and he became the new king of the Ostrogoths. In 484 AD he was elected as Roman Consul. By this time the Ostrogoths had multiplied to such an extent that the land around the Volga was not sufficient to supply their needs. It was becoming increasingly necessary to move elsewhere.

Meanwhile in Italy there was chaos. No enlightened leader had replaced Alaric. The invasion of Attila the Hun in 452 AD, followed by his death in Milan in 453 AD, had brought greater unrest to the north of Italy. The leaderless army he left behind was left to its own devices. The subsequent plunder of Rome by Genseric the Vandal in 455 AD caused equal turmoil in the south of Italy. Restlessness was everywhere. The country was torn in civil strife, and plagued by the exploitation and greed of the nobles and the intrigues of the Roman Catholic Church. Having suffered a temporary set-back during the reign of Alaric, this institution was now busily continuing to gain control in the land. The transfer of power and wealth into the hands of the Pope became increasingly marked. The decrees of religious tolerance which Alaric had made were withdrawn by the leader of Rome, under pressure from Pope Hilarius, in 467 AD.

The outward splendour of the papal court grew brighter as that of the Caesar's waned. The revenue from the Official Church's domains increased and it became, writes Scott, 'a satire on the general poverty of the city.' [1] As the life of the Roman citizens grew harder and poorer, the shrines of the Church's martyrs and saints grew with ever fresh splendour. Italy was full of unrest and discontent.

Out of this disorder a new leader named Odoacer emerged. He was a Gothic mercenary. He sent an embassy to Zeno, the Emperor of Constantinople, saying that Zeno should be the sole Emperor of the Roman Empire, and that he, Odoacer, would rule Italy. From this point the Western Empire had ceased to exist as such. Odoacer ruled from 476 to 490 AD, and in Rome at least there was a degree of order:

> Like the rest of the 'barbarians' he had been instructed in the 'Arian heresy'; but he revered the monastic and episcopal characters; and the silence of the Catholics attests the toleration which they enjoyed ... Italy was protected by the arms of its conqueror; and its frontiers were respected by the 'barbarians' of Gaul and Germany. [2]

However, beyond Rome the country of Italy was not at peace.

o   o   o   o   o

The Emperor Zeno in Constantinople regarded the crumbling Roman Empire with disquiet. To the north the Ostrogoths were becoming restless. To the west Italy was in turmoil. Whether as an act of wisdom or self-defence, he made Theodoric, the king of the Ostrogoths, a patrician and entrusted him with the mission of restoring order to Italy.

Thus it was with full imperial approval that Theodoric began the long and difficult march to Italy in the autumn of 488 AD. The journey was hard. They faced a march of 700 miles through the snows of winter. Theodoric marched at the head of 40,000 soldiers. Their wives and children and possessions followed behind them, drawn in wagons. They entered Italy in 489 AD.

By 493 AD Theodoric's conquest of Italy was complete. Odoacer was defeated and the Ostrogoths were distributed and settled all over Italy:

> A firm though gentle discipline imposed the habits of modesty, obedience and temperance; and the Goths were instructed to spare the people, to reverence the laws, to understand the duties of civil society, and to disclaim the barbarous licence of judicial combat and private revenge. [3]

To begin with, the other tribes in Europe viewed Theodoric's conquest with disquiet. When it became clear, however, that he intended to establish peace and worship of the One God in the land, their alarm was changed to respect. They accepted his powerful mediation, which was uniformly employed for the best purposes of reconciling their quarrels and settling their differences. His domestic alliances, a wife, two daughters, a sister, and a niece, united the family of Theodoric with the kings of the Franks, the Burgundians, the Visigoths, the Vandals, and the Thuringians; and contributed to maintain the harmony and the balance of central Europe.

Theodoric's rule, which lasted until 526 AD, was a time of great and generally diffused happiness for the people of Italy. The Pontine Marshes were drained, harbours were built and the burden of taxation was lightened. Italy's agriculture was so much improved that it ceased to import corn and began to export it. Such was the extraordinary plenty, which an industrious people produced from a grateful soil, that the merchants of the world were drawn to Italy. Their beneficial traffic was encouraged and protected by the liberal spirit of Theodoric, and travel throughout the provinces of Italy by land and water was restored and extended. The city gates were never shut either by day or night; and the common saying, that a purse of gold might be safely left in the fields, indicates the peace which pervaded Italy at this time.

Theodoric was a firm believer in the Arian faith, and his rule was moulded by the practical application of the knowledge and the way of life which Ulfilas had first brought to the Goths. His rule has been noted for his toleration of the Official Trinitarian Church, and he showed the greatest consideration towards the Roman Catholics. He believed that:

> We cannot impose a religion by command because no one can be compelled to believe against his will. [4]

Gibbon writes that:

> He justly conceived himself to be the guardian of the public worship; and his external reverence for a superstition which he despised, may have nourished in his mind the salutary indifference of a statesman or philosopher. The Catholics of his dominions acknowledged, perhaps with reluctance, the peace of the church; their clergy, according to the decrees of rank or merit, were honourably entertained in the palace of Theodoric. [5]

Such was his reputation for justice, that Theodoric was even asked to arbitrate between two rival candidates for the papacy, Symmachus and Laurence. His decision was accepted by both parties.

He also equally tolerated the practices of the Jews and defended them from malice and persecution. It is recorded that on one occasion he even enforced a general levy to compensate for the losses which some Jews had suffered in a riot. He was heavily criticised by the Official Trinitarian Church for doing this.

There was therefore during the reign of Theodoric a unified and peaceful Europe which was predominantly Arian in faith. And it was during his reign that Hilderic, who became the leader of the Vandals in 523 AD, restored the customary Arian toleration of the Official Roman Catholic Church in North Africa.

The Arian Empire, however, which at this time extended over much of southern Europe, including southern France, Spain and Italy, as well as over North Africa, was not safe from the designs of the Official Church. As in the case of Hilderic, it actively worked towards the downfall of Theodoric during the breathing space afforded by his toleration of this institution. Eventually the Arians were attacked from the East and from the West and from within.

As we have just seen in the last chapter, the Emperor Justinian issued his decree from Constantinople, in 523 AD, in which he exposed to persecution all who refused to accept the official Trinitarian religion, throughout the Roman Empire. Theodoric sent Pope John to Constantinople to request Justinian to annul his savage edicts. He claimed for his distressed brothers in the East the same indulgence which he had so long granted to the Catholics of his domains in the West. As in the case of Hunneric, who had been the leader of the Vandals before Hilderic, and who had also attempted to persuade the Roman Emperor to exercise religious toleration throughout the Roman Empire, the mission failed. Theodoric suspected that Pope John was guilty of double-dealing. He had him arrested and put in prison, where he died.

When news reached Theodoric of Justinian's continued persecution of the Unitarian Christians in the East, Theodoric could not check his feelings of anger, resentment and the desire for revenge:

> A mandate was prepared in Italy, to prohibit, after a stated day, the exercise of the Catholic worship. By the bigotry of his subjects and enemies, the most tolerant of princes was driven to the brink of persecution. [6]

The mandate, however, was neither published nor implemented, but the ill-feeling remained.

Theodoric was not only troubled by the persecution of Justinian in the East, but also by dissension from within. Boethius, the philosopher-king of Rome and champion of the Roman Catholics, began to stir up trouble in the Senate. He talked freely of the 'liberation of Rome' and caused unrest. Theodoric eventually imprisoned him, and finally killed him and his sympathiser, Symmachus, in 524 AD.

This action filled his heart with remorse, and unrest amongst the Official Trinitarian Christians grew. The Roman Catholics, angered by the death of Pope John, Boethius and Symmachus, renewed their efforts to be rid of the Arian ruler. The last two years of his reign were clouded by his own gloom and growing unrest in his kingdom.

Theodoric's policy of peaceful co-existence foundered because of the unrelenting opposition of the Roman Catholic Church. His tolerant rule was never appreciated by the Trinitarians, who were involved more with treading the corridors of power than travelling the way to their Lord.

Hodgkin writes that had Theodoric been a pagan, he would have been extolled, but because in the eyes of the Official Church he was a 'heretic', his best efforts were accepted with sullen distrust. From them he earned nothing but misapprehension, dislike and hatred. At the close of a glorious life, the king of Italy discovered that he had excited the hatred of a people whose happiness he had so assiduously laboured to promote. Theodoric died, full of remorse, in 526 AD. Gibbon, however, has only praise for Theodoric, King of the Ostrogoths. He describes him as:

> ... a hero, alike excellent in the arts of war and of government, who restored an age of peace and prosperity, and whose name still excites and deserves the attention of mankind. [7]

After the death of Theodoric, there followed thirty years of chaos during which the Official Trinitarian Church finally re-asserted itself in Italy. In order to understand more clearly how this happened, it is necessary briefly to examine the life of Clovis, King of the Franks.

o   o   o   o   o

The rule of Clovis coincided with that of Theodoric, King of the Ostrogoths. Supported by the Official Church, he attacked the Arian empire from the west at the same time as Justinian's attacks came from the east.

The Franks had always remained aloof from Christianity in whatever form. It was they who had combined with Attila the Hun in his battle against the Arian Visigoths at Chalons in 452 AD. During the reign of Clovis, however, which lasted from 481 to 511 AD, the Franks were converted to Trinitarian Catholicism.

Following the wishes and persuasion of his wife, Clotilda, Clovis became a Roman Catholic in 496 AD when he was thirty years old. He was baptised in the cathedral of Rheims in dramatic splendour, with a phial, the Sainte Ampoulle, of 'holy' oil, which was always used for the coronation of the kings of France, being brought down from the ceiling of the cathedral by a white dove:

> The new Constantine was immediately baptised, with three thousand of his warlike subjects: and their example was imitated by the remainder of the gentle barbarians who, in obedience, to the victorious prelate, adorned the cross which they had burnt, and burnt the idols which they had formerly adored. [8]

The Roman Catholic Church was overjoyed with the conversion of such a powerful king, for:

> On the memorable day, when Clovis ascended from the baptismal font, he alone, in the Christian world, deserved the name and prerogatives of a Catholic king ... the 'barbarians' of Italy, Africa, Spain and Gaul were involved in the Arian 'heresy'. The eldest, or rather the only son, of the church, was acknowledged by the clergy as their lawful sovereign, or glorious deliverer; and the arms of Clovis were strenuously supported by the zeal and favour of the Catholic faction. [9]

Strengthened by the allegiance of this powerful king, the Official Roman Catholic Church made large inroads into the Visigothic kingdom of southern France. The Visigoths there had enjoyed peace and prosperity for so long that they had neglected the arts of self-defence. They were unprepared for the sudden invasion which Clovis initiated in 507 AD. He marched south with his army and overtook the fleeing Visigothic army forty miles outside Poitiers. He challenged the king of the Visigoths, another Alaric, to single combat, and killed him. The Gothic army was then routed and massacred.

Clovis then continued his victorious march south into Aquitaine, and in the following years the Arian Visigoths were driven further and further south. These successful inroads into the Arian Empire were yet another source of concern to Theodoric, King of the Ostrogoths, during his reign in Italy. He had worked hard to unite Europe, and this source of disruption was indubitably another of the major reasons for the gloom in which he ended his reign.

The 'reconquest' of France by the Roman Catholic Church was completed with the final conquest of Burgundy by the Franks in 532 AD, led by the sons of Clovis. Anyone who refused to adopt the Trinitarian religion of the Franks thereafter was eliminated.

Once the Church had re-established itself in France, it began to extend its activities to the east and to the south, towards Italy and towards Spain. The Franks, under the auspices of the Roman Catholic Church invaded Italy in 538 AD, and destroyed Milan in 539 AD. Their movement down from the north-west coincided with that of Belisarius, the famous general of the Emperor Justinian, coming up from the south-east.

○   ○   ○   ○   ○

It will be remembered that Belisarius conquered Carthage, the capital of the Donatists and the Arian Vandals, in 533 AD, at the same time that the conquest of Visigothic Gaul was completed by the sons of Clovis. Having re-established the Official Church in Carthage, and having quelled all resistance from the Vandals, Belisarius left some of his army in Carthage and returned to Constantinople, where, as we have already seen, he handed over Gelimer, the leader of the Vandals to the Emperor Justinian.

Although Theodoric, King of the Ostrogoths, had been dead for seven years, the Ostrogoths were still powerful in Italy, and there was every chance that they would try and retake Carthage. Having committed himself to conquering North Africa, Justinian was bound to also conquer Sicily and Italy. This decision was supported by the insistence of the Roman Catholic Church and fuelled by his own hatred of anyone who affirmed the Divine Unity and denied the doctrine of Trinity. Accordingly the army of Belisarius was re-equipped and enlarged, and it set sail for Sicily in 536 AD.

As in the case of Alaric, King of the Visigoths, in Italy, so in the case of Theodoric, King of the Ostrogoths, no new leader of any worth emerged after his death. When Belisarius landed in Sicily, he met with little organised resistance, and he soon continued his journey to Naples. He took the city of Naples in 537 AD, and many people were killed. However, it appears that Belisarius was not only an outstanding general, but also a humane one and he did, as in his conquest of Carthage, attempt to moderate the calamities which he foresaw as being the inevitable companions of a victorious army, saying:

The gold and silver, are the just rewards of your valour. But spare the inhabitants, they are Christians, they are suppliants, they are now your fellow-subjects. Restore the children to their parents, the wives to their husbands; and show them, by your generosity, of what friends they have obstinately deprived themselves. [10]

Having wiped out any resistance in Naples, Belisarius marched on Rome. Theodatus, the new king of the Ostrogoths, capitulated without a fight. He acknowledged Justinian as Emperor and abdicated. Vitiges, a general of the Gothic army, retreated with his men to Ravenna where he prepared for war. Belisarius marched into Rome without a struggle.

In the spring of 537 AD, Vitiges laid siege to Rome, but without success. Belisarius resisted the siege and was sent reinforcements by Justinian. After a year and nine months, the siege was abandoned by the Goths, in March 538 AD, and they retreated to Ravenna. They had lost a third of their army, and as they withdrew Belisarius attacked, inflicting even greater losses.

In 539 AD, the same year that the Franks destroyed Milan, Belisarius captured Ravenna and took Vitiges prisoner. He was asked by Justinian to return to Constantinople with the booty, which he did, taking Vitiges with him.

Thus by the end of 539 AD, only thirteen years after the end of Theodoric's famous reign, the Official Trinitarian Christian armies had virtually reconquered the whole of Italy. Under the orders of the Emperor Justinian all the Arian churches were handed over to the Catholics, and under his edicts all those who refused to accept Trinitarian Christianity were killed or exiled.

This did not take place without a struggle. In the absence of Belisarius, Rome was retaken by the Goths. He was recalled, and retook the capital in 547 AD. He left, and the Goths again took Rome, in 549 AD. Narses was sent from Constantinople to reconquer Italy, which he did, retaking Rome in 562 AD.

From this time on, the Official Roman Catholic Church gained in strength, and all traces of the Arian Goths in Italy were systematically removed. The last group of Unitarian Christians to survive, in the very north of Italy, were the Lombards. They were 'converted' to the official religion in about 600 AD.

o   o   o   o   o

The survivors of the Ostrogoths were pushed westwards and, following the path of the Visigoths before them, they sought refuge in Spain. After the conquests of Clovis and his sons in France, and of Belisarius and his successors in Italy, Spain was the last remaining stronghold of the Arian Goths. It was only a matter of time before they too would cease to exist.

○   ○   ○   ○   ○

Chapter Six

The Goths
in the
Iberian Peninsula

The Arian Goths flourished in the Iberian peninsula during the fifth and sixth centuries AD, and their rule was characterised by their toleration of the Official Roman Catholic Church. This toleration of the Trinitarian Christians by those who affirmed the Divine Unity was a way of behaviour which nearly always characterised the Unitarian Christians whenever they were established in the land. Conversely, the intolerance displayed by the Official Trinitarian Church whenever it was in power nearly always characterised its behaviour towards anyone who disagreed with its version of Christianity, especially the Unitarian Christians. As with Alaric and Theodoric in Italy, so with the Arians in what is now Spain and Portugal, the Roman Catholic Church was not content to be tolerated and left alone. As its history shows, its aims were directed more towards achieving power on earth, than towards leading a life of harmony in accordance with the original guidance which had been revealed to Jesus, peace be on him, by his Creator.

The toleration extended by the Goths to the Roman Catholics allowed them to organise and subvert the Arians from within, while the successful Official Trinitarian Christian armies of France began to make inroads into the north of Spain from without. The situation was almost an exact blueprint of what was to occur towards the end of the Muslims' stay in Spain six hundred years later. Indeed the story of the Arian Goths in the Iberian peninsula, from beginning to end, is virtually the same story as that of the Muslims in Spain, the main difference being that the Goths came down from the north, whereas the Muslims came up from the south.

The account of the demise of the Arian Goths in Spain which follows is a short one, not only because reliable records scarcely exist, but also because the account of the Muslims' demise in Spain is more fully documented and therefore better illustrates the nature of this recurrent pattern more clearly, and demonstrates the mechanics of the Trinitarian persecution of Unitarians in Spain in more detail.

○   ○   ○   ○   ○

As in Italy, so in the Iberian peninsula, the Official Trinitarian Church did not rest until the Arians had either been eliminated or absorbed into the structure of the Roman Catholic Church. The advances of the Roman Catholic armies from the north diminished the territories which the Arians inhabited and ruled, whilst from within the Roman Catholics gradually insinuated their ways into the life-style of the rulers. As soon as the rulers began to wander from the guidance they had been following, the unity of the Arian community was breached, and it divided against itself. This sealed the end of the Arian Goths' peaceful rule in the Iberian peninsula.

The last Unitarian Christian king to rule Spain was Leovigilid. His son, Hermenegild, accepted Roman Catholicism and, with his eyes on the crown, rebelled against his father. The Suevi in the northwest of Spain had also recently adopted Roman Catholicism. Hermenegild united them with the invading army of the Franks, and between 577 and 584 AD they fought Leovigilid. Hermenegild was eventually heavily defeated and compelled to surrender. His father allowed him to continue to follow the Roman Catholic religion. Hermenegild abused this toleration and continued to plot against his father. Leovigilid therefore had his son executed.

Leovigilid's other son and successor was called Recared. Not wishing to share Hermenegild's fate, he waited until his father had died. Once he had been made king, he began to implement his policy of making Roman Catholicism the official religion of Spain, and there was a wave of persecution of the Arians between 586 and 589 AD. Recared publicly recognised the doctrines of the Roman Catholic Church as being the 'orthodox' religion in 587 AD, and Roman Catholicism was officially approved and confirmed as the state religion in the third Council of Toledo, in 589 AD.

As in the case of the Emperor Constantine, Recared's acceptance of the Catholic Church appears to have been based more on political expediency than on any firm conviction as to the truth of its doctrines: 'To recover sovereignty over a kingdom undivided,' writes Castro, 'was well worth renouncing the dogma of the nondivinity of Christ.' [1]

Recared's opening words in the Council of Toledo made it apparent that he considered himself the saviour of both the Iberian peninsula and of the Catholic Church. His manner is strongly reminiscent of the first decree of Theodosius:

> I do not believe that it is unknown to you that my object in calling you before the presence of Our Serenity is the re-establishment of the form of ecclesiastic discipline ... God (whom it has pleased to remove the obstacle of 'heresy' by means of us) has admonished us that we should restore the ecclesiastic custom. May you be filled with joy and gladness to know that through the providence of God the Canonical Custom has returned to the paternal precinct to Our Glory. [2]

Recared spoke as if he were doing a great favour to both God and the Roman Catholic Church. However it appears from his speech that his motives, if anything, were selfish, and it is clear that he had chosen this course of action, 'so that in the future our glory may shine, honoured by the testimony of the Catholic faith.' [3] Thus Recared principally regarded the religion of the Official Church as a means to further his own ambitions. Throughout his speech the Roman Catholic faith was only mentioned as a custom, ecclesiastical law, and liturgy, but not as a way of life:

> Whoever reads the minutes of the famous Council without any preconceptions will get the impression that political interest, reasons of state, take precedence over religious sentiments and worries about the future life. [4]

All that was necessary, as far as Recared was concerned, was to change a few words:

> Instead of saying, as had been the practice among the Visigoths, '*Gloria Patri per Filium in Spiritu Sancto*', now the priests were required to say, '*Gloria Patri et Filio et Spiritu Sancto*'. A dative instead of the accusative and all was in order. [5]

Thus instead of saying 'Glory be to the Father through the Son in the Holy Spirit', the people of Spain were persuaded to say, 'Glory be to the Father and to the Son and to the Holy Spirit'.

The subsequent pattern of events after the Third Council of Toledo was a repetition of the story of the Official Church's climb to power during the reigns of Constantine and Theodosius. Like Constantine before him, Recared wished to use the religion of the Official Church to unite his kingdom and to contain the powerful and seditious activities of a divided nobility. To begin with, he liked to appoint all bishops himself, and disliked any interference from the Official Church in these matters. There were a number of instances when he overruled the recommendations of the Official Church leaders, and made whomever he wanted a bishop. Like Theodosius before him, however, he ended up by being a servant of the Roman Catholic Church:

> The bishops did not confine themselves to moulding the hearts and minds of kings; they themselves undertook legislation and administration. They declared in their public records that they had been appointed, by the Lord Jesus Christ, guardians of the nation. Surrounded by his nobles, the king prostrated himself humbly before them when they were assembled in council at Toledo, and implored them with signs and tears to intercede to God on his behalf, and to give wise laws to the State. [6]

As in the rule of Theodosius, many of these 'wise laws' took the form of religious persecution. In the years that followed the Goths who held firmly to Unitarian Christianity were eliminated. Like Arius and his followers, they were rooted out with ruthless ferocity. The Goths were only allowed to exist on the condition that they accepted Roman Catholicism as their religion.

With the passage of time the Official Trinitarian Church and the rulers of the land became more and more identified with each other. They were corrupted by power and wealth, and once more the land was caught in a decaying and decadent feudal system:

> The clergy when they attained to power disavowed the principles which they had set forth when they were destitute ... Henceforth, possessed of vast domains densely populated with serfs, of splendid palaces crowded with slaves, the bishops recognised that they had been premature, that the time for emancipating the serfs was not yet, and might not arrive for centuries to come. [7]

The state of the country degenerated into a decay similar to the one which, as we have already seen, had existed immediately before the arrival of the Arian Visigoths in Spain. This was the state of the country just before the Muslims came. In both cases the advanced social decay of the society was accompanied by an almost total lack of the affirmation and worship of the Divine Unity by its members.

When the Muslims first arrived on the shores of North Africa nearest the Iberian peninsula, they came upon a few Arian Gothic settlements. These were inhabited by the descendants of the last of the Spanish Arian Goths who had either fled or been banished by the Roman Catholics to the shores of Africa.

o   o   o   o   o

Today there is no trace of the Arian Goths in either Thrace, Italy, France, Spain or Africa. They have left their mark on the art and architecture of Europe, but in spite of this they are almost universally described by the historians as 'barbarians', and the European histories are full of the tales of their alleged brutality. The fact that they affirmed and worshipped the Divine Unity is either ignored, or covered over by the use of vindictive euphemisms such as 'heretic' and 'schismatic'.

Yet undoubtedly the Goths were at one time one of the most civilised peoples to have lived in Europe. Charles Kingsley writes of the re-generative effect which they had on Europe, and of the sane influence of their way of life which involved:

> ... comparative purity of morals, sacred respect for women, for family life, for law, equal justice, individual freedom, and above all for honesty in word, and deed ... with hearts blessed with a strange willingness to learn. [8]

As long as they held to their Unitarian faith they were successful. When they left it, they perished. Their story stands out in the history of Europe. Nowhere, with the exception of the Muslims of Spain, was there an achievement so great or a downfall so complete. They have left their mark from the Bosphorus to the Pillars of Hercules (which once supported, it is said, a bridge that straddled Spain and North Africa), and viewed chronologically they form the link between the Roman Empire and Modern Europe – but they have completely disappeared. The majority of historians have done them no justice; all their books have been destroyed; and the majority of those who have written about them have been their enemies.

In spite of the fact that their record has been destroyed so effectively, the meagre fragments that have been discovered recently indicate the greatness, the vitality, the tenacity, the heroism and the initiative of the Arian Goths. It is impossible to write about them, however, without feeling a failure to have done them full justice. Their story has been covered up so effectively that in reading about them, one learns more about the contempt and bigotry of their enemies than of the Goths themselves.

Although much of what has been written about them is far from the truth, it is clear, however, that the Arian Goths flourished as long as they held to the teaching of Jesus which had been transmitted to them by Ulfilas. They were eventually destroyed because their leaders became corrupted and left that guidance and because, by doing so, they became vulnerable to the organised and systematic persecution which was always levelled against them by the Official Roman Catholic Church.

o   o   o   o   o

Chapter Seven

The Jews
in the
Iberian Peninsula

It is at this point in the history of the conflict between the Trinitarian and the Unitarian Christians in the Iberian peninsula that the history of the persecution of the Jews by the Official Roman Catholic Church in what is now called Spain and Portugal becomes relevant, although of course Jews had already been inhabiting the Iberian peninsula for centuries, and long before the coming of Jesus, peace be on him. According to Isaac de Pinto:

> When the other Jews were taken into the Babylonian captivity – in 586 BC – 'the chief families of Judah were sent to Spain' where the superior qualities of this Jewish elite were preserved for more than two thousand years.[1]

Some commentators are of the opinion that the reason why the persecution of the Jews has been a continued and world-wide phenomenon for virtually the last two millennia is that it is because they have not only rejected two Prophets of God, Jesus and Muhammad, peace be on them, but also have altered and abandoned the original guidance which was revealed to the Prophet Moses, peace be on him. As far as the Roman Catholic Church in the 7th century AD was concerned, however, the Jews, who persisted in believing in One God, were to be treated and punished like the Unitarian Christians, simply because they did not subscribe to the doctrine of Trinity; furthermore, since even the Trinitarian Church had not yet compromised the command of God not to indulge in usury, those Jews who nevertheless made a living from it were despised for it; and finally, since the Trinitarian Christians mistakenly believed not only that Jesus had been crucified, but also that it was the Jews who were largely responsible for the alleged crucifiction, they still tended to blindly hold all Jews responsible for it, even though several centuries and even more generations of Jews had since come and gone.

○ ○ ○ ○ ○

Once, as we have just seen in the last chapter, the Official Roman Catholic Church had established its power over the king in Spain towards the end of the sixth century AD, it became very rich. Having silenced the Arian Goths, the Official Church and the State, in reality the same body, undertook the persecution of the Jews living in the Iberian peninsula, and with unparalleled ferocity:

> Michelet justly observed, 'Whenever during the Middle Ages men began to ask how is it that the ideal Paradise of the world under the sway of the Church was realised here below as a Hell, the Church, conscious of the objection hastened to stifle it by declaring that, "It is the wrath of God. It is due to the crime of the Jews. The murderers of our Lord are still unpunished." And a persecution of Jews was set on foot.' [2]

In 616 AD, King Sisebut, a Catholic Goth, decreed that all Jews must be converted to Roman Catholicism before the end of the year. On expiry of this date all unconverted Jews were to be banished after receiving one hundred lashes. The Jews were forbidden to celebrate the Passover, or circumcision, or marriage according to the Jewish rites. Any Jew who failed to give his child a 'Christian' baptism was to receive a hundred lashes, forfeit his land to the King and have his head shaven for a sign.

As a result of this decree more than 90,000 Jews were baptised. They, however, constituted a minority of the Jewish population. Those who were baptised continued to practise circumcision and to follow all the Mosaic laws. For seventy years their persecution was carried out half-heartedly, but then there followed a period of concentrated attacks on the Jews:

> The fortunes of the obstinate 'infidels' were confiscated, their bodies were tortured; and it seems doubtful whether they were permitted to abandon their native

country. The excessive zeal of the Catholic king was moderated, even by the clergy of Spain, who solemnly pronounced an inconsistent sentence: that the sacraments should not be forcibly imposed, but that the Jews who had been baptised should be constrained, for the honour of the Church to persevere in the external practice of a religion which they disbelieved and detested. Their frequent relapses provoked one of the successors of Sisebut to banish the whole nation from his dominions; and a council of Toledo published a decree, that every Gothic king should swear to maintain this salutary edict. [3]

In 681 AD, the Council of Toledo again decreed that they should either be baptised or expelled, and the majority of Jews were forcibly baptised, since it was made virtually impossible for them to leave the country. A decree of 693 AD made it impossible for the Jews to function as merchants. In 694 AD, it was decreed that all unconverted Jews were to be sold into slavery, except children under seven, who were to be brought up as Christians.

This last decree was too much for the Jews, and in the same year, seventeen years before the conquest of Spain by the Muslims, they revolted. The plan was that all the exiled Jews who had found refuge on the other side of the Straits of Gibraltar were to attack Spain. As soon as they landed, the Jews already in Spain were to revolt simultaneously in all the places where they were strongest. The king's spies found out about the revolt, however, and it was mercilessly put down by the simple expedient of killing the majority of able-bodied Jews in Spain. Those who survived the general massacre, were condemned to slavery. Old Jews were generally allowed to retain their religion, but the young were henceforth brought up in the Christian faith. Marriages between Jews were forbidden, and a Jewish slave was only allowed to marry a Christian slave.

In this manner the Jewish community in Spain was greatly diminished, disrupted, divided and deprived of its property. This relentless persecution of the Jews added to the general unrest which permeated Spain on the eve of the Muslims' arrival. The country was smothered in a decaying and corrupt feudal system. The slaves and the serfs were overburdened. The middle class citizens had to bear the brunt of the taxes, since the nobles and the clergy were exempt from such liabilities. Instead these privileged classes were engaged in the quest for pleasure and power. They had no forces with which to oppose an invasion except those of the serfs and the Jewish slaves. Understandably there was little love between the rulers and the ruled at this time, and it is not surprising that both the Jews and the serfs, and many of the impoverished citizens, actively helped the Muslims overcome their tyrannical rulers:

> The Gothic kings and bishops at length discovered that injuries will produce hatred, and that hatred will find the opportunity of revenge. A nation, the secret or professed enemies of Christianity, still multiplied in servitude and distress; and the intrigues of the Jews promoted the rapid success of the Arabian conquerors. [4]

The oppressed majority of this corrupt and decaying society regarded the Muslims not so much as conquerors but more as saviours. The Muslims ended their slavery and gave them freedom to practise their religion. The country was ripe and ready for the new injection of life which came with the Muslims when they landed in the south of Spain during the summer of 711 AD, only 92 years after the Prophet Muhammad, blessings and peace be on him, had journeyed to Madina al-Munawarra, 'the Illuminated City', and begun to establish the way of Islam in it. One of the meanings of the Arabic word, '*Andalus*', is 'to become green at the end of summer'. This was certainly the reality of that summer in which the Muslims first came to Spain.

o   o   o   o   o

Chapter Eight
The Early Paulicians

Before examining the history of the Muslims in Spain, or Andalus, as the Muslims call it, it would be illuminating to examine the history of the fresh wave of Unitarian Christianity which reached its peak in the Eastern Roman Empire at the very time that the last of the Arian Goths were being eliminated from Spain in the West. The people involved in this movement were originally called the Paulicians.

◉   ◉   ◉   ◉   ◉

The Paulicians were originally the followers of Paul of Samosata, who was a Nazarene. He was taught by Diodorus, the leader of the Nazarene Church in Antioch after the apostles of Jesus had died. He was one of the purest transmitters of the original teaching of Jesus. Paul of Samosata's followers included Lucian who taught Arius, and Eusebius of Nicomedia who taught Ulfilas the Goth. He also greatly influenced Nestorius, whose Unitarian followers spread as far east as India and China, and as far south as Abyssinia. He was thus an essential link in the chain of transmission, which had started with Jesus and then spread up to Antioch and beyond through Barnabas and his followers. It was through them that the affirmation and worship of the Divine Unity spread right across Europe and right across North Africa in two separate movements which, as we have already seen in Chapter Four, culminated in their reunion when the Arian Vandals of Europe came down through Spain and settled in North Africa after linking up with the Arians and the Donatists who were already there.

As well as these movements to the West, the original teaching of Jesus was also taken to the East. The group of the followers of Paul of Samosata, who were first known as the Paulinians but who later became known as the Paulicians, initially settled in the provinces of Asia Minor to the west of the Euphrates. For the next ten centuries they were systematically persecuted wherever their movement spread, and their books were almost completely destroyed.

To begin with, much of the Paulician's teaching was transmitted orally, and accordingly there was always the danger that this wisdom would be wiped out along with the men who possessed it. During the eighth century, however, their teaching flourished throughout Thrace, and even the Emperor of Constantinople at this time, Constantine the Adoptionist, was a Unitarian Christian. During his reign the leaders of the Paulicians were summoned to the Imperial Court and those parts of the oral tradition which could be reduced to written form were recorded on paper. The book that resulted was called *The Key of Truth*.

Nearly all copies of this book were subsequently destroyed during the following centuries. However, a man called Frederic Conybeare came across an early manuscript of *The Key of Truth* while travelling in Armenia during the mid-nineteenth century. He had a copy made of it and translated it. Thanks to his work a considerable amount of information which had been buried for centuries was made available to the public.

The Key of Truth presents a picture of a Unitarian Christian Church based on completely different lines to the Roman Catholic Church, both in doctrine and worship. Before the publication of this book there had only been a limited and officially censored version of the activities of the Paulicians. Now we know much more about their rites and disciplines, and their general organisation, as well as having a far more complete knowledge of their beliefs and tenets. *The Key of Truth* thus gives a far more accurate and just description of the earliest form of Unitarian Christianity than that provided by the Official Trinitarian Church:

> A lost Church rises before our eyes, not a dead anatomy
> but a living organism ... We can, as it were, enter the
> humble congregation, be present at the simple rites, and
> find ourselves at home among the worshippers. [1]

It is significant that the communities of the Paulicians lacked any form of organised priesthood:

> The Paulician teachers were distinguished only by their
> scriptural names, by the modest title of fellow-pilgrims,
> by the austerity of their lives, their zeal or knowledge,
> and the credit of some extraordinary gifts of the holy
> spirit. But they were incapable of desiring, or at least of

obtaining, the wealth and honours of the Catholic pre-
lacy. Such anti-Christian pride they bitterly censured;
and even the rank of elders or presbyters was condemned as an institution of the Jewish synagogue. [2]

The leaders of the Paulicians were chosen on account of their knowledge of the teachings of Jesus, peace be on him, but there was no
hierarchy of higher and lower clergy, for they believed that, 'God
giveth not the spirit by measure.' [3] Their leaders were all married
and had children. They lived in the way that the closest followers
of Jesus had lived. They described themselves as belonging to the
holy, universal and apostolic church founded by Jesus. They pre-
served all the apostolic traditions which Jesus had revealed to his
closest followers, including the practice of worshipping and then
eating together. Their 'communion service' was no more than this.
They had no doctrine of transubstantiation, which claims that the
bread and the wine which the Official Trinitarian Christians share
is changed into the 'body and blood' of Christ, even though they
still look and taste the same.

The Paulicians had no visible object of worship. They affirmed
the Divine Unity. They were not dualists as their enemies have insinuated, for it was the common practice of the Official Christians
to associate them with the Manichaeans, yet another sect of the
early Christians who compromised the teaching of Jesus with the
dualistic philosophy of the Magian fire-worshippers who followed
Zoroaster, and who believed that God and Satan were conflicting
opposites – in opposition to the teaching of all of the true Prophets
of God who have always taught that God is the Creator of both
good and evil, and that while He has power over both – including
Satan – yet He cannot be associated with any thing.

The Paulicians had their own gospel, which was not one of the
four official gospels. They made a clear distinction between the
Old Testament and their own gospel:

Since they adored the latter as the oracles of God, and
abhorred the former as the fabulous and absurd invention of men and daemons. [4]

Another of their books was *The Shepherd of Hermas*, which was written between 88 and 97 AD at Patmos near Ephesus, long before the
official *New Testament* canon was fixed. *The Shepherd* was accepted

as a revealed book by the Nazarenes, and was forbidden by the Official Roman Catholic Church. It was virtually lost to the world until a third century papyrus manuscript of the text was discovered in 1922:

> It was found that the Greek used by Hermas was a simple vernacular. The language could be understood by the common people and it is clear that the book was written for everyone and not just for an intellectual elite. His style was frank and informal and he possessed an originality of expression which made the book easy to read.
>
> Hermas begins by telling of four visions he experienced, the last of which he calls a revelation since on this occasion an angel visited him dressed as a shepherd. The angel informed Hermas that he had been sent by the 'most reverend angel' (that is, the angel Gabriel), to live with Hermas for the rest of the days of his life.
>
> The angel then ordered Hermas to write down all 'the Commands and the Parables.' Since these were dictated to him by the angel, who only related what he was told to say by the 'most reverend angel', *The Shepherd* was accepted as a revealed book by the earlier Christians. [5]

The first command is a clear affirmation of the Divine Unity:

> First of all believe that God is One and that He created all things and organised them, and out of what did not exist made all things to be, and He contains all things but Alone is Himself uncontained. Trust Him therefore and fear Him, and, fearing Him, be self-controlled. Keep this command and you will cast away from yourself all wickedness, put on every virtue of uprightness, and you will live to God if you keep this commandment. [6]

It is very probable that the Paulicians also used the *Didache*, which was a Nazarene manual of behaviour and church procedure. It was written in the language spoken by the poor people, and was clearly addressed not only to learned men, but to everyone. It was written between 60 and 160 AD, and it has been established that to some extent it relied on the writings of Barnabas:

Part of the *Didache* has been borrowed from the earlier
part of the *Epistle of Barnabas*. [7]

Harnack, the famous Christologist, and subsequently Bishop John
Wordsworth, are both of the view that the author of the *Didache*
did not regard St. Paul and St. Luke as authoritative. As with nearly
all other Unitarian Christian writings the *Didache* has been virtually destroyed. Only fragments remain. Their context indicates that
the lost pages contained material which revealed the abuses of the
Official Church.

In the light of such censorship Conybeare's discovery and translation of the manuscript of *The Key of Truth* is vitally illuminating.
It is especially revealing in its description of Jesus and his nature.

The Paulicians affirmed that Jesus was a man and a Prophet,
peace be on him, but not God. They therefore respected the Virgin
Mary and believed in the immaculate conception, but did not think
of her as somehow being 'the mother of God'. They did not say
that Jesus was born on the twenty-fifth of December, since this belief only originated in Rome towards the end of the fourth century,
when the celebration of his birth was grafted on to one of the old
pagan winter solstice festivals.

The Paulicians said that Jesus was born a human being and remained one. They therefore had no doctrine of Incarnation, the doctrine by which the Official Trinitarian Church tried to explain that
God could also be a man at the same time. Instead the Paulicians
said that Jesus, because of his moral excellence, was favoured and
chosen by God. When he was baptised by John at the age of thirty
he was given knowledge from God by means of the Holy Spirit,
that is, the angel Gabriel. He was thus endowed with the authority
and lordship over men which enabled him to serve them.

Competent authorities have acknowledged that this Christology
does not contradict the synoptic gospels. This view agrees with
chapter forty-eight of Justin Martyr's *Dialogue*, where the author,
in spite of his rejection of the doctrine recorded in *The Key of Truth*,
agrees that the 'basis' of its teaching is the same as his. He admits
that the concept of the 'divinity of Christ' rests on a 'prophetic'
rather than a historical basis, but fails to add that the source of this
'prophetic basis' was not a Prophet, but Paul of Tarsus. He further
agrees that it is more reasonable to envisage that Jesus was born a
human being and was then anointed by way of election: 'For we
all,' he says, 'expect the Messiah to be born a man of men.' [8]

It was because of this belief that the Paulicians were some times known as 'Adoptionists'. This school, which can be traced back to Byzantium in about 185 AD, was led by a man called Theodatus. He affirmed the immaculate conception, but denied the 'divinity' of Jesus. He said that Jesus was a man imbued with the inspiration of the Holy Spirit from his baptism. He had thus attained such perfection of holiness that he was 'adopted' by God as his 'son'. Theodatus, whose views were accepted by Paul of Samosata, was excommunicated by the Official Trinitarian Church in about 195 AD.

Following the example of Jesus, the Paulicians did not practise infant baptism, which had never been taught by him, and which they regarded as an innovation, an innovation which in fact was not finally accepted into the Roman Catholic Church until the Council of Trent in the sixteenth century. The members of the Paulician communities were baptised when they had reached a mature age. There was no compulsion in their rites of baptism. They said that true baptism should be preceded by repentance and true faith if it was to have any meaning.

The Paulicians did not subscribe to the doctrine of the Trinity in the least, and even the word 'trinity' was entirely foreign to their teachings. They rejected the doctrine as being unscriptural, and as having been borrowed from the Platonic system of philosophy. The *Logos* is nowhere mentioned in *The Key of Truth*. Paul of Samosata dismissed the use of such terminology as an innovation which would not enlighten but only mystify.

The certainty of the Paulicians as to the nature of Jesus and the nature of God could only be the fruit of pure teaching. It is possible that their gospel, which was not one of the four officially accepted gospels, may well have been the *Gospel of Barnabas*. This gospel, one of the three hundred which were almost utterly destroyed by the Official Trinitarian Church after the Council of Nicaea, clearly distinguishes between Jesus and God.

Although it cannot be established with any degree of certainty whether or not the sixteenth century Italian version of *The Gospel of Barnabas* is a faithful translation of the original – to which frequent reference is often made in the writings of the early Christian fathers, but which apparently no longer exists – any more than it can be established whether or not any of the *post* Council of Nicea Greek and Latin versions of the four officially accepted Gospels are faithful translations of the original Aramaic or Hebrew versions which also used to exist but apparently no longer exist – the following

excerpt from the English translation of the Italian version by
Lonsdale and Laura Ragg gives a clear indication of the differences
that existed between Unitarian and Trinitarian doctrine. It describes
what is alleged to have taken place immediately before the miraculous feeding of the five thousand – an account which, as well
as furnishing an explanation as to why such a large crowd had
gathered in the first place, cannot be found in the four officially
accepted Gospels, and for obvious reasons, since it describes how
Jesus publicly demonstrated that he could not possibly be identified with God, simply by comparing his human attributes with
God's divine attributes:

> Accordingly the governor and the priest and the king
> prayed Jesus that in order to quiet the people he should
> mount up into a lofty place and speak to the people.
> Then went up Jesus on to one of the twelve stones which
> Joshua made the twelve tribes take up from the midst
> of Jordan, when all Israel passed over there dry shod;
> and he said with a loud voice: 'Let our priest go up into
> a high place whence he may confirm my words.'
>
> Thereupon the priest went up thither; to whom Jesus
> said distinctly, so that everyone might hear: 'It is writ-
> ten in the testament and covenant of the living God that
> our God has no beginning; neither shall He ever have
> an end.'
>
> The priest answered: 'Even so it is written therein.'
>
> Jesus said: 'It is written there that our God by His
> word alone has created all things.'
>
> 'Even so it is,' said the priest.
>
> Jesus said: 'It is written there that God is invisible
> and hidden from the mind of man, seeing He is incor-
> poreal and uncomposed, without variableness.'
>
> 'So is it truly,' said the priest.
>
> Jesus said: 'It is written there how that the heaven of
> heavens cannot contain Him, seeing that our God is in-
> finite.'
>
> 'So said Solomon the Prophet,' said the priest, 'O Je-
> sus.'
>
> Said Jesus: 'It is written there that God has no need,
> forasmuch as He eats not, sleeps not, and suffers not
> from any deficiency.'
>
> 'So is it,' said the priest.

Said Jesus: 'It is written there that our God is every-where, and that there is not any other god but He, Who strikes down and makes whole, and does all that pleases Him.'

'So is it written,' replied the priest.

Then Jesus, having lifted up his hands, said: 'Lord our God, this is my faith wherewith I shall come to Your judgement: in testimony against every one that shall believe the contrary.'

And turning himself towards the people, he said, 'Repent, for from all that of which the priest has said that it is written in the book of Moses, the covenant of God for ever, you may perceive your sin; for that I am a visible man and a morsel of clay that walks upon the earth, mortal as are other men. And I have had a beginning, and shall have an end, and am such that I cannot create a fly over again.'

Thereupon the people raised their voices weeping, and said, 'We have sinned, Lord our God, against You; have mercy upon us.' And they prayed Jesus, every one, that he would pray for the safety of the holy city, that our God in his anger should not give it over to be trod-den down of the nations. Thereupon Jesus, having lifted up his hands, prayed for the holy city and for the peo-ple of God, every one crying, 'So be it, Amen.' (*The Gospel of Barnabas: 95*).

Clearly anyone who had access to teaching such as this could not possibly confuse Jesus with God. The certainty which the Pauli-cians possessed regarding this fundamental matter indicates that their gospel, whether it was the *Gospel of Barnabas* or not, must have contained the same, or a similar, doctrine.

The Paulicians also confirmed that it was not Jesus who was crucified, but another man in his place. They therefore regarded the story of the resurrection as a fiction, and rejected the mythical doctrine of the Atonement and Redemption of Sins which Paul of Tarsus had invented. Similarly, the Paulicians had no doctrine of Original Sin. In view of this, they naturally rejected the symbol shared by the Official Church and the Roman sun-god, the cross, as having no spiritual significance. They regarded all images of

Jesus or Mary, whether painted or carved, as idolatrous and alien to the teaching of Jesus and contrary to the second commandment contained in the *Old Testament*. It was forbidden even to make a sign of the cross.

Instead the Paulicians held to the original teaching of Jesus, peace be on him, as best they could. There was no pomp or show in their liturgy and worship and, like the Ebionites in Syria, they were ridiculed for their simplicity and for their poverty, which was based on the living example of Jesus. The basis of their life was that there was no object worthy of worship other than the One God, and that it was Jesus, peace be on him, who had taught people how to worship Him. The Paulicians believed that whoever believed in his teaching and sought to embody it as he had done would receive grace and favour from God in both this world and the next. The inner dimension of their teaching must have been completely hidden from those who ridiculed and persecuted them, for it was to free the soul from the cage of the body, and to truly understand existence.

○   ○   ○   ○   ○

Persecution followed the teaching of the Paulicians wherever it took root. The vow which the leaders of the Paulicians made when they were elected, included the undertaking that they were prepared:

> ... to take on themselves scourgings, imprisonments, tortures, reproaches, crosses, blows, tribulations and all the temptations of the world. [9]

The Paulicians suffered under the early persecution of the Christians by the Romans, and were one of the groups who were condemned by the Council of Nicaea in 325 AD. Persecution after this date increased. In 417 AD, the Official Trinitarian Church held a council at Shahapivan, and it was decided, in the twentieth canon, that all Paulicians were to be branded on the forehead with the image of a fox. Anyone who left the Church and joined a community of Paulicians was to be hamstrung. This general persecution drove the Paulicians northwards into Armenia where they flourished and became known as the Armenian Church. Conybeare states that according to manuscripts in the Bodleian Library, the Adoptionists, or Paulicians, who went from Antioch to Armenia, are described as people who were clothed in sack-cloth, barefooted and ascetic in their lives. They preached against the worship of the cross. Among the names mentioned, one Theodore is prominent.

By the middle of the fifth century AD, the Paulicians' way of life was widespread in south-east Armenia:

> ... it not only attracted bishops, priests, deacons and monks but native satraps, princes, feudal lords, and headmen of villages with their entire families ... [10]

And with the passage of time the Paulicians' way of life became the national life-style of Armenia, and even spread into southern Russia.

During the fifth century AD, however, the Romans began to extend their empire into Armenia. Wherever the imperial army went, there too was the Official Trinitarian Church. The Paulicians were tortured and killed and driven out of that part of Armenia which came under the rule of Constantinople. However, many Paulicians survived by fleeing further east, or to the south. During the rapid spread of Islam in the last half of the seventh century, many of them recognised that this was a revelation confirming the one which they were following, and they embraced Islam.

There was no compulsion in the matter, and many Paulicians, whilst making an alliance with the Muslims, preferred to keep their separate identity. Thus Conybeare remarks that several centuries later the Latin Crusaders found the Paulicians always fighting on the side of the Muslims, but remaining a distinct group of people. Pope Clement addressing Charles V is recorded as saying that the religion of Paul of Samosata was, 'nothing different from pure Mohammatanism.' [11]

It is of course likely that the gospel which the Paulicians used still contained references to the coming of the Prophet Muhammad, blessings and peace be on him, which would not only confirm the affinity between the teachings of the Paulicians and the Muslims, but also explain the ease with which the Paulicians recognised and embraced Islam when they came into contact with the Muslims.

It is certainly confirmed by the *Qur'an* that both Moses and Jesus did tell their respective followers about the coming of the Prophet Muhammad, blessings and peace be on them, and many of the three hundred gospels which were destroyed after the Council of Nicaea in 325 AD by the Official Roman Catholic Church must have contained explicit references to what Jesus had said about this. Whereas there are only a few indirect references to the coming of the Prophet Muhammad left in John's Gospel, the last and the least authentic of the gospels to be written, in which its author refers to the coming of 'the Paraclete' or 'the Comforter', there are, for example, several clear references to the coming of the Prophet Muhammad in the *Gospel of Barnabas*, which, as we have already seen, may well have been the gospel used by the Paulicians.

It is interesting to note in this context that in these references, the author of the *Gospel of Barnabas* states that Jesus said that he was not the Messiah, but rather that the Prophet Muhammad was the Messiah, blessings and peace be on both of them. Since the *Qur'an* confirms that Jesus was indeed the Messiah, the accusation levelled by the Official Trinitarian Church that the Italian version of the *Gospel of Barnabas* is a forgery written by a Christian scholar who converted to Islam in the sixteenth century appears somewhat odd, since even a simple Muslim would be unlikely to make such a simple mistake.

If the Italian version of the *Gospel of Barnabas* had been forged by a Muslim – which is highly unlikely in any event – who had intimate knowledge of the *Bible* as well as of the *Qur'an*, then he or she would have been far more inclined to refer to Muhammad as 'the Paraclete', or 'the Comforter', blessings and peace be on him, than to describe him as 'the Messiah', the epithet reserved exclusively in the *Qur'an* to describe Jesus, peace be on him.

Furthermore, as well as containing material which is virtually identical to some of the contents of the four officially accepted gospels, the *Gospel of Barnabas* also contains a great deal of material which does not contradict the four officially accepted gospels, but which is not to be found either in the *Old Testament*, or in the *Qur'an*, or in the *Hadith*, the verified records of what the Prophet Muhammad was seen to have said and done transmitted by his companions. This question accordingly arises: 'If the Italian version of the *Gospel of Barnabas* is a forgery, then who or what is the source of this additional material? If it is not a forgery, then of course this question does not arise.

Again, although it is impossible to verify the contents of the Italian version of the *Gospel of Barnabas*, just as it is impossible to verify the contents of the four officially accepted canonical gospels contained in the *New Testament* – since in each case there is no original manuscript with which any comparison can be made – it is nevertheless interesting to consider the contents of the following passage which is taken from the English translation of the Italian version of the *Gospel of Barnabas,* and which its author states is a personal eye-witness account of what was said after the interrogation of Jesus which, as we have just seen, took place before the miraculous feeding of the five thousand:

> When the prayer was ended, the priest said with a loud voice, 'Stay, Jesus, for we need to know who you are, for the quieting of our nation.'
>
> Jesus answered, 'I am Jesus, son of Mary, of the seed of David, a man that is mortal and fears God, and I seek that to God be given honour and glory.'
>
> The priest answered, 'In the book of Moses it is written that our God must send us the Messiah, who shall come to announce to us that which God wills, and shall bring to the world the mercy of God. Therefore I pray you tell us the truth, are you the Messiah of God whom we expect?'
>
> Jesus answered, 'It is true that God has so promised, but indeed I am not he, for he is made before me, and shall come after me.'
>
> The priest answered, 'By your words and signs at any rate we believe you to be a Prophet and a holy one of God, wherefore I pray you in the name of all Judea and Israel that you for love of God should tell us in what wise the Messiah will come.'
>
> Jesus answered, 'As God lives, in Whose presence my soul stands, I am not the Messiah whom all the tribes of the earth expect, even as God promised to our father Abraham, saying, "In your seed will I bless all the tribes of the earth." But when God shall take me away from the world, Satan will raise again this accursed sedition, by making the impious believe that I am God and son of God, whence my words and my doctrine shall be contaminated, insomuch that scarcely shall there remain thirty faithful ones: whereupon God will have mercy

upon the world, and will send His Messenger for whom
He has made all things; who shall come from the south
with power, and shall destroy the idols with the idola-
ters; who shall take away the dominion from Satan
which he has over men. He shall bring with him the
mercy of God for salvation of them that shall believe in
him, and blessed is he who shall believe his words.

'Unworthy though I am to untie his hosen, I have received grace and mercy from God to see him.'

Then answered the priest, with the governor and the
king, saying, 'Distress not your self, O Jesus, holy one
of God, because in our time shall not this sedition be
any more, seeing that we will write to the sacred Roman senate in such wise that by imperial decree none
shall any more call thee God or son of God.'

Then said Jesus, 'With your words I am not consoled,
because where you hope for light darkness shall come;
but my consolation is in the coming of the Messenger,
who shall destroy every false opinion of me, and his
faith shall spread and shall take hold of the whole world,
for so has God promised to Abraham our father. And
that which gives me consolation is that his faith shall
have no end, but shall be kept inviolate by God.'

The priest answered, 'After the coming of the Messenger of God shall other prophets come?'

Jesus answered, 'There shall not come after him true
prophets sent by God, but there shall come a great number of false prophets, whereat I sorrow. For Satan shall
raise them up by the just judgement of God, and they
shall hide themselves under the pretext of my gospel.'

Herod answered, 'How is it a just judgement of God
that such impious men should come?'

Jesus answered, 'It is just that he who will not believe in the truth to his salvation should believe in a lie
to his damnation. Wherefore I say unto you, that the
world has ever despised the true prophets and loved
the false, as can be seen in the time of Michaiah and
Jeremiah. For every like loves his like.'

Then said the priest, 'How shall the Messiah be called,
and what sign shall reveal his coming?'

Jesus answered, 'The name of the Messiah is admirable, for God Himself gave him the name when He had created his soul, and placed it in a celestial splendour. God said, "Wait Muhammad; for for your sake I will to create Paradise, the world, and a great multitude of creatures, whereof I make you a present, insomuch that whoso shall bless you shall be blessed, and whoso shall curse you shall be accursed. When I shall send you into the world I shall send you as my Messenger of salvation, and your word shall be true, insomuch that heaven and earth shall fail, but your faith shall never fail." Muhammad is his blessed name.'

Then the crowd lifted up their voices, saying, 'O God, send us Your Messenger: O Muhammad, come quickly for the salvation of the world!' (*The Gospel of Barnabas: 96-97*).

If both the original *Gospel of Barnabas* and at least some of the other Unitarian Christian gospels which were so ruthlessly suppressed and destroyed after the Council of Nicaea in 325 AD – including the gospel used by the Paulicians – contained passages such as this, then this goes a long way towards explaining the sustained persecution of the Unitarian Christians by the Trinitarian Christians – especially after the coming of the Prophet Muhammad, blessings and peace be on him, as foretold – for clearly the respective doctrines of the Trinitarians and the Unitarians were and are mutually incompatible.

It is not known whether or not the gospel of the Paulicians was the *Gospel of Barnabas*, for all their gospels have been destroyed. It is however probable that many of the other gospels banned by the Official Roman Catholic Church were just as explicit, and that one of these three hundred gospels was that of the Paulicians. Clearly these gospels did not do anything towards bolstering up the framework of the Official Trinitarian Church, and this was why they and those who read and believed them were so ruthlessly destroyed.

The affinity between the teachings of the Paulicians and of the Muslims indicates the purity of the Paulicians' way of life. Their respective Prophets, Jesus and Muhammad, both brought the same fundamental teaching, and both derived their knowledge from the same and only source, God.

The main difference between the two is that whereas both Moses and Jesus, peace be on them, were sent specifically to the twelve tribes of the Tribe of Israel, Muhammad, blessings and peace be on him, was sent with a teaching for *all* people. It is clear that the teachings of both Moses and Jesus were dramatically altered once they filtered through to people who did not belong to the Tribe of Israel – especially the European Jews (the Khazars) and the European Christians – and accordingly it is impossible not to reach the conclusion that although the teachings of the Unitarian Christians in Europe were far closer to the original teachings of Jesus than the teachings of the Trinitarian Christians, even the teachings of the Unitarian Christians, and accordingly their way of life, could not have entirely corresponded with what Jesus originally brought. And God knows best.

Furthermore, it is clear that by the end of the seventh century AD, the original teachings of Jesus had already been lost, not only by the Trinitarian and Unitarian Christians in Europe, but even by the Unitarian Christians who were members of the Tribe of Israel:

> As far as the original followers of Jesus are concerned, access to the Prophetic way of life through Jesus had been lost by the end of the 7th century AD, for with the coming of the Prophet Muhammad, may God bless him and grant him peace – who died in 632 AD after delivering his message and establishing the way of Islam as a living social reality – the last of the relatively few Christians who still had access to the original teachings of Jesus, peace be on him, recognised the Prophet whose coming Jesus had foretold and embraced Islam. [12]

Nevertheless, not all of those who professed to be following Jesus followed this example, and inevitably the religions of both Unitarian and Trinitarian Christianity continued to exist and interact, both with each other and with others, colouring the lives and daily existence of countless people in the process.

○   ○   ○   ○   ○

Returning to the history of the Paulicians in the late seventh and early eighth centuries AD, we find that, as in the case of the other Christian Unitarians, much of the history of the Paulicians has been suppressed in the official histories and can only be traced by the brief references made to their continued persecution. Thus, for example, one of the events mentioned by Gibbon is the stoning to death of Sylvanus, a leader of the Paulicians who was captured together with several of his companions by a man called Simeon:

> By a refinement of cruelty, Simeon placed the unfortunate Sylvanus before a line of his disciples, who were commanded, as the price of their pardon, and the proof of their repentance, to massacre their spiritual father. They turned aside from the impious office; the stones dropped from their filial hands, and of the whole number only one executioner could be found, a new David, as he is styled by the Catholics. [13]

It is recorded that this display of loyalty deeply affected Simeon, who later joined the Paulicians and was then himself martyred.

Despite continued persecution the Paulicians maintained their way of life, and their lot was improved when another emperor called Constantine, who was a Unitarian and an Adoptionist, became the ruler of Constantinople in the middle of the eighth century. Early on in his reign he made an expedition into Armenia, and found in the cities of Melitene and Theodosiopolis a great number of Paulicians. He persuaded many of them to return with him. They accordingly left the banks of the Euphrates and came to Constantinople and Thrace. Thus it was that the Unitarian Paulicians moved into the lands where the Unitarian Goths had once flourished some four centuries before.

It was by this emigration that the Paulicians' way of life was eventually introduced and diffused into Europe. During the rule of Constantine the Adoptionist, their way of life spread rapidly throughout Thrace. It was at his insistence that *The Key of Truth* came to be written.

Thus at the time when the last of the Unitarian Goths had been destroyed in what is now called Spain and Portugal, and when the Muslims had just arrived there, there was a fresh flowering of Unitarian Christianity in the East. In the years that followed, these Unitarian Paulicians were either to spread north and west with their teaching, or to embrace the way of Islam which came up so rapidly from the south.

The rule of Constantine the Adoptionist, called Catallinus by John of Damascus, was a tumultuous one. He actively opposed the innovations of the Official Church, and consequently there was conflict between the two. He rejected infant baptism, and indeed it is said that he fouled the font of St. Sophia when Germanus the Patriarch was baptising him as a child! He is especially noted and remembered for his campaign against the worship of saints and their relics, and the worship of images, by the Official Christians. In order to appreciate the significance of this campaign, especially in relation to the history of the Paulicians, it is necessary to briefly explain how these practices first arose.

O   O   O   O   O

The earliest followers of Jesus would have nothing to do with image worship:

> The primitive Christians were possessed with an unconquerable repugnance to the use and abuse of images, and this aversion may be ascribed to their descent from the Jews, and their enmity to the Greeks. The Mosaic law had severely proscribed all representations of the Deity; and that precept was firmly established, in the principles and practice of the chosen people. [14]

All the early Christian fathers, including Clement and Tertullian, condemned image worship as being contrary to the second commandment of the *Old Testament* which clearly forbids making any representation of any living thing. It reads:

> Thou shalt not make unto thee any graven image, or any likeness of any thing that is in heaven above, or that is in the earth beneath, or that is in the water under the earth; thou shalt not bow down thyself to them, nor serve them: for I the Lord thy God am a jealous God, visiting the iniquity of the fathers upon the children unto the third and fourth generation of them that hate Me; and showing mercy unto thousands of them that love Me, and keep My commandments. (*Exodus 20: 4-6*).

When Jesus came, he taught the same doctrine as Moses, peace be on them, and for the first two centuries after his death none of his followers indulged in what is today euphemistically referred to as 'sacred art'.

The introduction of images into the Official Christian Church, when it did come, was literally an underground movement. It began in the catacombs. As early as the third century emblems such as a shepherd, a lamb, a fish, a dove, a cock, or a ship were scratched or painted on the rock surrounding the tomb. With the passage of time this 'art' became more ambitious and scenes such as Abraham about to sacrifice Isaac were depicted in the catacombs. All the subject matter was taken from the *Old Testament*. No attempt was made to represent the likeness of Jesus until the reign of the Emperor Constantine 'the Great' in the early fourth century, when, as we have already seen in Chapter Two, the representation of the cross also became very popular.

During the reign of Constantine the Great, and especially after the Council of Nicaea in 325 AD, the practice of 'religious art' received official approval for the first time. It not only became more ambitious in its subject matter, but also crept up from the catacombs and into the churches themselves, to take equal place with the veneration of the remains of holy Christians who had died:

> The first introduction of a symbolic worship was in the veneration of the cross, and of relics ... But a memorial, more interesting than the skull or the sandals of a departed worthy, is a faithful copy of his person and features, delineated by the arts of painting or sculpture ... At first the experiment was made with caution and scruple; and the venerable pictures were discreetly allowed to instruct the ignorant, to awaken the cold, and to gratify the prejudices of the heathen proselytes. By a slow though inevitable progression, the honours of the original were transferred to the copy: the devout Christian prayed before the image of a saint: and the pagan rites of genuflexion, luminaries, and incense, again stole into the Catholic Church. [15]

However, these practices were not accepted overnight, and were bitterly opposed by the Nazarene school of Christians including the Arians, the Donatists and the early Paulicians. In 326 AD, for example, Eusebius of Nicomedia heatedly replied to a request from Constantina, the sister of the Emperor Constantine, to send her a likeness of Christ, with these uncompromising words:

> What and what kind of likeness of Christ is there? Such images are forbidden by the second commandment. [16]

However, not only the painting of pictures, but also the displaying of reverence towards them, were firmly established, at least in the Official Trinitarian Churches by the end of the fourth century AD. Basil, who died in 379 AD, is recorded as saying about them:

> I reverence and kiss them with homage ... as they are not forbidden but are painted on all our Churches. [17]

During the following two centuries, the practice became widespread in the Official Roman Catholic Church:

> The use, and even the worship, of images, was firmly established before the end of the sixth century ... the Parthenon and Vatican were adorned with the emblems of a new superstition; but this semblance of idolatry was more coldly entertained by the 'rude barbarians' and the Arian clergy of the West. [18]

The main 'religious artists' at this time were the monks who made a considerable amount of money from the works of their hands and the ignorance of the people. Perhaps their most ingenious invention was the 'Edessa', a handkerchief which had purportedly been offered to Jesus to wipe his brow during his supposed journey to the place of his alleged crucifixion. It was said that when he was supposed to have removed the handkerchief from his brow, the delineations of his face were left imprinted on it. This handkerchief was fabricated five centuries after Jesus had left the earth, in the town of Edessa, from whence it received its name. It was reverenced as the source of many miracles and military victories. Indeed it was so successful that many similar 'originals' – including perhaps the Turin shroud, which has received so much publicity in recent years – were made and sold all over the Roman Empire:

Before the end of the sixth century, these images 'made without hand' (in Greek it is a single word), were propagated in the camps and cities of the eastern Empire; they were the objects of worship, and the instruments of miracles; and in the hour of danger or tumult their venerable presence could revive the hope, rekindle the courage, or repress the fury, of the Roman legions. [19]

Naturally these practices only found favour with those who had either abandoned the original teaching of Jesus, peace be on him, or who had never come into contact with it in the first place. Those who held to it avoided them:

As the worship of images had never been established by any general or positive law, its progress in the eastern empire had been retarded, or accelerated, by the differences of men and manners ... The splendid devotion was fondly cherished by the levity of the capital, and the inventive genius of the Byzantine clergy, while the rude and remote districts of Asia were strangers to this innovation of sacred luxury. Many large congregations of Gnostics and Arians maintained, after their conversion the simple worship which had preceded their separation; and the Armenians, the most warlike subjects of Rome, were not reconciled, in the twelfth century, to the sight of images. [20]

During the sixth and seventh centuries AD, the worship of the Virgin Mary and the saints, their visions and miracles, their relics and images, were preached by the monks and worshipped by the people. It was not until the Paulicians – who, it will be remembered, had begun to move from further east into Thrace in the seventh century and who were established there in the eighth – began to have some influence that any serious attempt was made to check this innovation.

Leo the Iconoclast began the destruction of images in Constantinople in 726 AD. He met with vigorous opposition, not only in Constantinople but also from Rome, and some of the letters written to him by Pope Gregory II are still extant. The Pope had nothing but good words for image-worship. In one of his letters he said that these images were, 'the genuine forms of Christ, his mother, and his saints, who had approved, by a crowd of miracles, the innocence and merit of this relative worship.' Gibbon comments:

> He must indeed have trusted to the ignorance of Leo since he could assert the perpetual use of images, from the apostolic age, and their venerable presence in the six synods of the Catholic Church. [21]

Leo was unimpressed by the Pope's arguments and continued to smash idols. He prepared to extend his activities to Italy itself. Gregory II wrote him a stern warning:

> Are you ignorant that the popes are the bond of union, the mediators of peace between the east and west? The eyes of the nations are fixed on our humility; and they revere, as a god upon earth, the apostle St. Peter, whose image you threaten to destroy ... Abandon your rash and fatal enterprise; reflect, tremble, and repent. If you persist, we are innocent of the blood that will be spilt in the contest; may it fall upon your own head. [22]

Leo ignored the Pope's warning, and the whole of Italy prepared for his threatened invasion. The Italians swore to live and die in the defence of the Pope and the holy images. Leo's army landed in Italy and attacked Ravenna where it was heavily defeated. The waters of the Po were so deeply infected with blood that for six years no one would eat the fish of the river. An annual feast was instituted to celebrate the victory over Leo's army, and the worship of images in Italy continued unabated. Pope Gregory II pronounced a general excommunication against all who by word or deed should attack the tradition of the official Church fathers and the images of the saints. There was thus a quite definite split made between the Roman and Byzantine churches, which continues until today.

When Leo's son, Constantine the Adoptionist, became emperor of the eastern Empire, he continued his father's work in and around Constantinople. As we have already seen, it was he who was responsible for having *The Key of Truth* put into writing, and the Unitarian Christian Paulicians' way of life flourished during his reign.

In 754 AD, Constantine the Adoptionist called the Synod of Constantinople. It was attended by 338 bishops of Europe and Anatolia. None of the official Roman Catholic bishops from Rome attended, since Gregory II's general excommunication still placed the Greek Church beyond the Roman Catholics' definition of 'Christianity'. The Pope declared that the Greek Church had gone astray, and that its gatherings should be boycotted unless or until it returned to the norm of the Roman Catholic Church.

The synod attempted, in some degree, to re-establish the original teaching of Jesus:

> This Byzantine synod assumed the rank and powers of the Seventh General Council; yet even this title was a recognition of the six preceding assemblies which had laboriously built the structure of the Catholic faith. After a serious deliberation of six months, the 338 bishops pronounced and subscribed a unanimous decree, that all visible symbols of Christ except in the eucharist, were either blasphemous or heretical; that image-worship was a corruption of Christianity and a renewal of paganism; that all such monuments of idolatry should be broken or erased; and that those who should refuse to deliver the objects of their private superstition, were guilty of disobedience to the authority of the Church and of the Emperor. [23]

The results of this edict were tumultuous. The Roman Catholic Church and especially the monks, whose profession and even dress were also banned, strongly resisted this assault on their dignity and their income, and the remainder of Constantine the Adoptionist's reign was a stormy one.

The strenuous attempts of the Official Trinitarian Church to re-instate image-worship in Constantinople eventually proved successful during the rule of the Empress Irene. She decreed, in 780 AD, that image-worship was permissible within the Official Christian Church, and so once more the 'official religion' was re-asserted in the eastern Empire:

> 'The fond alliance of the monks and females,' writes Gibbon, 'obtained a final victory over the reason and authority of man.' [24]

This decree was followed by the second Council of Nicea, which was held in 787 AD. Since this council was held under the auspices of the Roman Catholic Church, Pope Hadrian sent some delegates from Rome. In all, three hundred and fifty bishops attended. After due deliberation, they formally re-established the Official Trinitarian Church's doctrine concerning image-worship:

> They unanimously pronounced, that the worship of images is agreeable to Scripture and reason, to the fathers and councils of the Church: but they hesitate whether that worship be relative or direct; whether the godhead, and the figure of Christ, be entitled to the same mode of adoration. Of this second Nicene Council, the acts are still extant; a curious monument of superstition and ignorance, of falsehood and folly ... For the honour of orthodoxy, at least the orthodoxy of the Roman Church, it is somewhat unfortunate, that the two princes who convened the two councils of Nice, are both stained with the blood of their sons. [25]

For the next sixty years the Official Roman Catholic Church struggled to make the Council's decision a reality throughout the Eastern Empire. Success finally came during the reign of the Empress Theodora who firmly established image-worship in Constantinople by about 842 AD. It was during her reign that another major confrontation between the Official Trinitarian Church and the Unitarian Paulicians took place, for the Paulicians would still have nothing to do with image-worship:

> The objects which had been transformed by the magic of superstition, appeared to the eyes of the Paulicians in their genuine and naked colours. An image made without hands, was the common workmanship of a mortal artist, to whose skill alone the wood and canvas must be indebted for their merit or value. The miraculous relics were a heap of bones and ashes, destitute of life or virtue, or of any relation, perhaps, with the person to whom they were ascribed. The true and vivifying cross was a piece of sound or rotten timber; the body and blood of Christ, a loaf of bread and a cup of wine, the gifts of nature and the symbols of grace. [26]

The confrontation between the Paulicians and the Official Trinitarian Church was a bloody one, and Gibbon was amazed at:

> ... the sanguinary devotion of Theodora, who restored the images to the oriental church. Her inquisitors explored the cities and mountains of the Lesser Asia, and the flatterers of the empress have affirmed, that, in a short reign, one hundred thousand Paulicians were extirpated by the sword, the gibbet, or the flames. [27]

Chapter Nine

The Later Paulicians

The widespread persecution instituted by Theodora in the ninth century AD drove the Paulicians of Armenia and Thrace to unite and fight back, and it is not surprising that the persecution by the Official Trinitarian Church strengthened their alliance with the Muslims. Many Paulicians embraced Islam as a result of this renewed contact with them. Others, however, continued to maintain their separate identity as Unitarian Christians.

The Paulicians were helped by the revolt of a soldier called Carbeas who commanded the guards of the general of the east. After his father had been impaled by some Roman Catholic inquisitors, he and five thousand of his men renounced their allegiance to the Roman Emperor and the official religion, and joined forces with the Muslims. In the mountains beyond Sewas and Trebizond, he founded and fortified the city of Tephrice, and all the Paulician fugitives who had taken to the hills gathered round him.

Between 845 and 880 AD, the combined forces of the Muslims and the Paulicians fought back against their would-be persecutors, and they won many victories. Even the dissolute Michael, the son of Theodora, was compelled to march against the Paulicians. He was defeated under the walls of Samosata, where the teacher of the first Paulicians had once lived, and the Roman Emperor fled before the 'heretics' whom his mother had condemned to the flames. The Muslims fought side by side with Carbeas, but the victory was ascribed to him.

Carbeas was succeeded by a man called Chrysocheir, an even greater and more daring leader. He boldly penetrated into the heart of Asia Minor with the Muslims, and the Official Christian army suffered many defeats at his hands:

> The troops of the frontier and the palace were repeat-
> edly overthrown, the edicts of persecution were an-
> swered by the pillage of Nicaea and Nicomedia, of

> Ancyra and Ephesus ... It is not unpleasing to observe
> the triumph of rebellion over the same despotism which
> has disdained the prayers of an injured people. [1]

When the Emperor Basil came to power, he tried to persuade Chrysocheir to settle down peacefully by means of bribery. When this failed, he renewed the campaign against the Paulicians. He met with some victories on the plains, but could not subdue Tephrice and the Paulicians in the mountains surrounding it. He returned to Constantinople and prayed for success. It was his daily prayer that he might live to pierce Chrysocheir's head with three arrows. His prayer was granted. After a successful inroad, Chrysocheir was surprised and slain in the retreat. His severed head was brought before the Emperor, who delightedly called for his bow and discharged three arrows into it, amidst general applause from his courtiers.

With the death of Chrysocheir, the glory of the Paulicians in Thrace faded and withered. The Emperor Basil mounted a second expedition to conquer Tephrice, and this time he was successful. The Paulicians who lived there either died fighting, or surrendered, or took refuge in the surrounding country:

> The city was ruined, but the spirit of independence survived in the mountains: the Paulicians defended, above
> a century, their religion and liberty. [2]

Although some remained in Thrace, a large number of Paulicians were driven northwards by the persecution of the Official Church, and they moved into Bulgaria. Following the same pattern of events as when the Paulicians had first moved into Armenia, and then into Thrace, their way of life was soon accepted by the majority of its population with enthusiasm.

The Paulicians of Bulgaria became known as 'the Bogomiles', for it was always the policy of the Official Church to change the name of the Paulicians whenever they reappeared in another country in order to cover over the unity and continuity of their movement. Inevitably the Paulicians of Bulgaria initially met with some persecution, but generally they were welcomed, and their movement spread rapidly. It followed the same direction as the Arian Goths had taken four centuries earlier:

The Bulgarians ... spread their branches over the face of Europe. United in common hatred of idolatry and Rome, they were connected by a form of episcopal and presbyterian government; their various sects were discriminated by some fainter or darker shades of theology; but they generally agreed on two principles, the contempt of the *Old Testament*, and the denial of the body of Christ, either on the cross or in the eucharist. A confession of simple worship and blameless manners is extorted from their enemies, and so high was their standard of perfection, that the increasing congregations were divided into two classes of disciples, of those who practised, and of those who aspired. [3]

Their example was so markedly different to that of the Trinitarian Christians, that many people embraced their way of life:

The favour and success of the Paulicians in the eleventh and twelfth centuries must be imputed to the strong though secret discontent which armed the most pious Christians against the Church of Rome. Her avarice was oppressive, her despotism odious; less degenerate perhaps than the Greeks in the worship of saints and images, her innovations were more rapid and scandalous; she had rigorously defined and imposed the doctrine of transubstantiation; the lives of the Latin clergy were more corrupt, and the eastern bishops might pass for the successors of the apostles if they were compared with the lordly prelates, who wielded by turns the crozier, the sceptre, and the sword. [4]

With the rapid expansion of the Paulicians came persecution from the Official Church, and they were harried wherever they settled. Their leader in Bulgaria was burnt alive in 1110 AD. Some of them who had migrated to Serbia were persecuted during the period around 1180 AD. Those who had settled in Bosnia and Herzegovina ably defended themselves, and when the Turkish Muslims eventually settled in these countries in 1463 and 1482 AD respectively, most of their Unitarian Christian descendants embraced Islam. Thus the origins of the present religious conflict in the Balkans can be traced right back to these ancient conflicts between the Trinitarian Christians on the one hand, and the Unitarian Christians and the Muslims on the other.

The main movement of the Paulicians which was launched from Bulgaria, and which was largely the result of the persecution which took place there, however, was directed beyond the Balkans, and towards central Europe.

A group of Paulicians migrated to southern Germany where they became known as 'the Catharii', which means 'the Pure'. Their movement spread further westwards and many of them settled in the south of France, around Toulouse especially, the same area which the Arian Goths had once ruled. They also spread down into the north of Italy. As well as the journeys made overland, many of the Paulicians from Bulgaria travelled by sea. They landed in Venice, in Sicily and in the south of France.

The Roman Catholic Church viewed their rapid growth with dismay. The Paulician Catharii were condemned by the Official Church as early as 1022, in the Council of Orleans. By the middle of the twelfth century, Catharian groups and churches were established throughout Europe, despite persecution. At this stage the Roman Catholic Church was so corrupt that it could not act efficiently and effectively. It was reduced to verbal opposition, and the Catharii were repeatedly condemned, as the Councils of Lombard in 1165, and of Verona in 1184, bear witness.

It was not until the next century that the Official Roman Catholic Church was able to organise any efficient means of persecution. However, it made up for its delay by initiating a drive against the Unitarian Christians of such dimensions as had not been witnessed for centuries.

> It was in the country of the Albigeois, in the southern provinces of France, that the Paulicians were most deeply implanted; and the same vicissitudes of martyrdom and revenge which had been displayed in the neighbourhood of the Euphrates, were repeated in the thirteenth century on the banks of the Rhone. The laws of the eastern Emperors were revived by Frederic II. The insurgents of Tephrice were represented by the barons and cities of Languedoc. Pope Innocent III surpassed the sanguinary notoriety of Theodora. It was in cruelty

alone that her soldiers could equal the heroes of the
Crusades, and the cruelty of her priests was far excelled
by the founders of the Inquisition; an office more
adopted to confirm, than to refute, the belief of an evil
principle ... The visible assemblies of the Paulicians, or
Albigeois, were extirpated by fire and sword; and the
bleeding remnant escaped by flight, concealment, or
Catholic conformity. But the invincible spirit which they
had kindled still lived and breathed in the western
world. [5]

    ○   ○   ○   ○   ○

Before examining the Mediaeval Inquisition and its destruction of
the Paulician Catharii in greater detail, it is important to remember that whatever the different names used to describe the
Paulicians during different periods and in different places, theirs
was a single and unified living movement. Like a plant, the seed of
their teaching was continually sown, grown, flowered, fruited,
withered, and almost dead – only to take root and spring up elsewhere. The process was a dynamic one, providing a striking con-
trast to the Official Church's attempts to formulate and then impose a rigid structure of institutionalised orthodoxy on life.

The movement of the Paulicians was so extensive that it cannot
be given the coverage it deserves in this present work. Wherever
the reader comes across accounts of 'the destruction of heretics' in
other historical works, however, if they do not describe the persecution of the Arians or the Donatists, then they are quite probably
describing the persecution of a group of the Paulicians, or of a group
of people who were influenced by them, whatever they may be
called by the historian in question.

The Nestorian Church, for example, was greatly influenced by
the teaching which was transmitted through Paul of Samosata and
the Paulicians. It spread as far east as China and eventually spread
back the way it had come. Under the rule of the Muslim Khalifs,
who tolerated anyone who wished to practise Christianity in peace,
the Nestorian Church was diffused from China to Jerusalem and
Cyprus. Their numbers, with those of the Jacobites who were another Christian sect, were computed to surpass the members of the
Greek and Latin Official Churches. Unitarian Christians flourished
under the protection of the Muslims, wherever they were.

    ○   ○   ○   ○   ○

The Nestorian Church was also well-established further afield. In Malabar, in India, they united with the followers of St. Thomas who is reputed to be buried near Madras. They were hardly bothered by anyone until the sea routes to the East were opened up in the sixteenth century AD:

> When the Portuguese first opened the navigation of India, the Christians of St. Thomas had been seated for ages on the coast of Malabar ... Their religion would have rendered them the firmest and most cordial allies of the Portuguese, but the Inquisitors soon discerned in the Christians of St. Thomas, the unpardonable guilt of a 'heresy' ... Instead of owning themselves the subjects of the Roman Pontiff, the spiritual and temporal monarch of the globe, they adhered, like their ancestors, to the communion of the Nestorian patriarch ... They united their adoration of the two persons of Christ; the title of Mother of God was offensive to their ear, and they measured with scrupulous avarice the honours of the Virgin Mary, whom the superstition of the Latins had almost exalted to the rank of a goddess. When her image was first presented to the disciples of St. Thomas, they indignantly exclaimed, 'We are Christians, not idolaters!' ... Their separation from the western world had left them in ignorance of the improvements or corruptions of a thousand years. [6]

The leaders of the Nestorian Church in Malabar were promptly killed by drowning, and the remainder were 'converted' to Roman Catholicism by the Jesuits, whose leader was Alexes de Menezes. After sixty years the Portuguese official clergy were driven out, and the Nestorian pattern of worship was re-established.

    ❍   ❍   ❍   ❍   ❍

A similar story is revealed about the Nestorian Church in Abyssinia. The Jesuits first arrived there in 1557, and in 1626 their leader, Alphonso Mendez, 'converted' the Abyssinian emperor and his subjects to the official religion of Rome:

> A new baptism, a new ordination, was inflicted on the natives; and they trembled with horror when the most

holy of the dead were torn from their graves, when the
most illustrious of the living were excommunicated by
a foreign priest. In the defence of their religion and their
liberty, the Abyssinians rose in arms, with desperate but
unsuccessful zeal. Five rebellions were extinguished in
the blood of the insurgents ... neither merit, nor rank,
nor sex, could save from an ignominious death the enemies of Rome. [7]

The Jesuits, however, were finally driven from Abyssinia, and its
Christian inhabitants returned to Unitarian worship.

     ◉   ◉   ◉   ◉   ◉

It is also quite possible that some of the first Christians in Great
Britain were Paulicians, although it is more likely that they were
Arians. During the reign of Theodosius, for example, two Arian
bishops, who were followers of Priscillian in Spain, were, as we
have already seen in Chapter Two, banished to the isles of Scilly.
Worship of the Divine Unity in Great Britain may well have spread
through them, or by means of other earlier Unitarian exiles or missionaries.

Certainly the first form of Christianity in Great Britain was Unitarian, and England was one of the last European countries to be
colonised by the Official Roman Catholic Church. As we have already seen in Chapter One, Roman Catholicism was not well established in the British Isles until the late seventh century AD,
largely as a result of the efforts of St. Augustine of Canterbury, and
only after the Synod of Whitby in 664 AD.

Most official histories of Britain, such as that of the venerable
Bede, who was a Trinitarian Christian, describe the inhabitants of
the British Isles prior to the mission of St. Augustine at the end of
the sixth century AD as 'pagans' and 'barbarians', although it is
clear from the works of historians such as Toland that in fact many
of them were Unitarian Christians.

Toland's description of the Unitarian Christians of Ireland in
his book, *Nazarenus*, for example, bears a marked resemblance to
the description of the Paulicians whose ways are described in *The
Key of Truth*. Toland says that the first Christians in Ireland believed
in One God, and not in the doctrine of the Trinity. There were no
images in their places of worship. They had no doctrine of transubstantiation. They had no doctrine of confession, and believed

that no one had the power to absolve wrong actions except God. Their gospel was written in their native tongue, and was not one of the four gospels officially approved by the Official Church. Their saints were not the same as those of the Official Trinitarian Church, and they were not canonised. Their marriage ceremonies did not necessarily take place in a church. There was no doctrine of celibacy. All their leaders married and had families. They practised temperance at all times, and usually ate only once a day. They regarded their Church not as a political empire, nor as an organisation, but as a congregation of faithful men and women who were present throughout the world. They called themselves the children of the Church.

When the first Roman Catholic missionaries arrived in Ireland, they predictably denounced the Irish Unitarian Christians as 'pagans' and 'heretics', and set about changing their way of life. The chief leader of the Catholic missionaries was called Patrick, who lived from 390 to 460 AD. His success is demonstrated by the fact that today he is ironically regarded as the apostle and patron saint of Ireland. He was in fact largely responsible for destroying the Celtic Unitarian Christian Church in Ireland, and for burning more than three hundred Celtic gospels. No Irish Unitarian gospel exists today. As with the Gothic alphabet, the Gaelic alphabet is no longer truly alive today.

By the time of the Synod of Whitby in 664 AD, the Celtic Unitarian Church in the British Isles had already been successfully 'catholicised', but although many of its members now subscribed to the doctrine of Trinity and mistakenly believed that Jesus had been crucified, there were still some differences between the Celtic Catholic Church and the Roman Catholic Church, notably as regards the manner in which the date for the feast of Easter should be calculated, the practice of infant baptism and tonsure-style.

Having listened to the arguments of the representatives for both parties, the king of Northumbria, King Oswin – who in the tradition of the Emperor Constantine at the Council of Nicea was presiding over the synod – decided in favour of Roman Catholicism on the basis of the passage in *Matthew 16: 18-19* which, as we have already seen in Chapter Two, had always been used by the Roman Catholic Church to support the claim that the Church in Rome was based on the teachings of Peter, who was to be given the keys to the kingdom of heaven. According to the venerable Bede, who describes the proceedings at the Synod of Whitby:

He said, 'Do you both agree, without any dispute, that these words were addressed primarily to Peter and that the Lord gave him the keys of the kingdom of heaven?'

They both answered, 'Yes.'

Thereupon the king concluded, 'Then I tell you, since he is the doorkeeper I will not contradict him; but I intend to obey his commands in everything to the best of my knowledge and ability, otherwise when I come to the gates of the kingdom of heaven, there may be no one to open them because the one who on your own showing holds the keys has turned his back on me.'

When the king had spoken, all who were seated there or standing by, both high and low, signified their assent, gave up their imperfect rules, and readily accepted in their place those which they recognised to be better. [8]

In this manner, the venerable Bede describes the settling of minor differences within the Official Catholic Church, but never once alludes to the major differences that existed between the Unitarian and Trinitarian Christians in Great Britain. His history provides a good example of what characterises an 'official history': as with so many other official histories like it, although it appears to be an impartial and scholarly work, anyone who relied solely on it would never even dream that there was once a thriving Celtic Unitarian Christian Church in the British Isles!

And as modern studies on the beginnings of Christianity have now firmly established, *none* of the four officially accepted gospels are eye-witness accounts written by companions of Jesus. As we have already seen, and as Dr. Maurice Bucaille points out:

As far as the decades following Jesus's mission are concerned, it must be understood that events did not at all happen in the way they have been said to have taken place and that Peter's arrival in Rome in no way laid the foundations for the Church. On the contrary, from the time Jesus left earth to the second half of the Second Century, there was a struggle between two factions. One was what one might call Pauline Christianity and the other Judeo-Christianity. It was only very slowly that the first supplanted the second, and Pauline Christianity triumphed over Judeo-Christianity. [9]

Given the nature and history of this struggle, and the complete lack of a *pre* Council of Nicea original manuscript of the Gospel of Matthew, it is extremely doubtful whether the passage in *Matthew 16: 18-19*, on which the Official Roman Catholic Church has always based its alleged authenticity and its claim that it must be obeyed – and on which King Oswin based his decision to adopt Roman Catholicism as the state religion for the British Isles – deserves the reliance which has been placed in it. This certainly appears to have been the position of King Henry VIII, who after being granted the title of 'Defender of the Faith' by the Pope in 1521, subsequently discarded Roman Catholicism as the state religion.

     o   o   o   o   o

These three brief examples of the Unitarian Churches in Malabar, Abyssinia and the British Isles, also indicate the probable limits of the extent of the influence of the Paulicians. However, as we have seen, their main activity was in and around Asia Minor and southern Europe, and it was there that they were persecuted most severely of all:

> Theirs the tears, theirs the blood shed during more than ten centuries of fierce persecution in the East. And if we reckon of their number as well as we may the early puritans of Europe, then the tale of wicked deeds wrought by the persecuting Churches reaches dimensions which appal the mind.
>
> As it was all done nominally out of reverence for, but in reality in mockery of, the Prince of Peace, it is hard to say of the Inquisition that they knew not what they did. [10]

To appreciate the extent of this fresh outbreak of persecution by the Official Trinitarian Church against the Paulician Unitarians of France and Italy, it is necessary to examine the structure of the Mediaeval version of the Inquisition, and to see how effectively it was rebuilt along the lines of the Inquisitions of Theodosius, Justinian and Theodora. This study is also vital if the reader is to appreciate the origins of the Spanish Inquisition, which stemmed from the Mediaeval Inquisition, and which was responsible for ensuring the extermination of virtually all the Jews and the Muslims of Spain during the sixteenth and seventeenth centuries.

     o   o   o   o   o

Chapter Ten

The End
of the
Paulicians

Up until the arrival of the Paulician Catharii in central Europe during the eleventh and twelfth centuries AD, the persecution of 'heretics' had not been organised on a large scale since the elimination of the Arian Goths several centuries before. The Official Trinitarian Church had grown so powerful that few people dared to openly differ from the tenets of its religion. With that power, however, came corruption, and with that corruption came enervation, and in the midst of this decay the fresh and living teaching of the Paulicians was eagerly accepted, took root and thrived.

Perhaps the most corrupt element in the Official Church at this time was that of the monks. Their movement had been started not by Jesus, peace be on him, but by St. Antony, in Egypt, three hundred years after Jesus had left the earth. His practices spread rapidly through the Official Christian world, and the monks divided into two classes, those who lived a solitary life and those who formed monastic communities and lived under a common and regular discipline. Initially the movement was an attempt to rediscover the original way of life of Jesus. However, many of them subscribed to the doctrines of the Official Church, and like this institution, once they accumulated wealth they were corrupted:

> As long as they maintained their original fervour, they approved themselves the faithful and benevolent stewards of the charity which was entrusted to their care. But their discipline was corrupted by prosperity; they gradually assumed the pride of wealth, and at last indulged the luxury of expense. Their public luxury might be excused by the magnificence of religious worship,

and the decent motive of erecting durable habitations for an immortal society. But every age of the church has accused the licentiousness of the degenerate monks; who no longer remembered the object of their institution, embraced the vain and sensual pleasures of the world, which they had renounced, and scandalously abused the riches which had been acquired by the austere virtues of their founders. [1]

To begin with the monks were predominantly in the eastern half of the Roman Empire. They made a lucrative living out of fabricating and selling images and relics and, as we have already seen in Chapter Eight, they were largely responsible for the popularity of image-worship within the Official Christian Church. They soon spread westwards into southern Europe, bringing their practices with them. The majority of their new followers became equally powerful and equally corrupt. Gibbon writes:

I have somewhere heard or read the frank confession of a Benedictine abbot: 'My vow of poverty has given me a hundred thousand crowns a year; my vow of obedience has raised me to the rank of a sovereign prince.' I forget the consequence of his vow of chastity. [2]

It was in the face of such corruption that the movement of the Paulician Catharii achieved such popularity. Theirs was by no means the only Unitarian movement to spring out of the decay of the Official Catholic Church in France. Another prominent group of people who rejected the dogma of the Trinitarian Church were the Waldenses.

The Waldenses were named after Peter Waldo, a rich merchant of Lyons who lived in the twelfth century. He had a *New Testament* translated into Romance, and a collection of extracts from the writings of the early Christian Fathers, known as 'sentences'. He studied these and learnt them by heart. He arrived at the conviction that nowhere was anyone living as Jesus had lived. He gave his land to his wife, sold his property, put his daughters in an abbey and gave what money was left to the poor. Having disposed of all his assets, he went preaching everywhere, and soon had a large following of men and women:

They entered houses announcing the gospel to the in-
mates; they preached in the churches, they discoursed
in the public places, and everywhere they found eager
listeners, for the negligence and indulgence of the clergy
had rendered the function of preaching almost a forgotten duty. [3]

The Waldenses wore robes and sandals, emulating Jesus, and became known as the 'Poor Men of Lyons'. They soon met with opposition from the Official Roman Catholic Church, for they refused
to worship Jesus as God, and they refused obedience to the authority of the Pope and his prelates since according to the apostles,
they said, God is to be obeyed rather than man.

They said that the concept of purgatory, and the costly masses
and alms which the clergy commissioned from people with the
promise of avoiding it, and the lucrative sacrament of confession
which enabled priests to extort money in return for granting for-
giveness and dispensations and indulgences, and indeed the priesthood itself – all of these, they said, were inventions of man and not
taught by Jesus. The Waldenses also said that women could preach,
and they held that prayer and remembrance of God in bed, or in a
room, or in a stable was as efficacious and as acceptable to God as
in a church.

In about 1190, the 'Poor Men of Lyons' united with the Paulician
Catharii. Their numbers were now so large that the Official Roman
Catholic Church was in danger of being superseded and replaced
by them. They all affirmed and worshipped the Divine Unity, and
rejected the whole structure of the priesthood of the Official Trinitarian Church as an innovation, for they knew that every human
being has direct access to God. They had their own gospels, written in Romance. These were accessible to all who wished to read
them, which was very popular with the people who, under the
rule of the Roman Catholic Church, had very little access even to
the official gospels.

The Official Trinitarian Church of this age literally kept its *Bibles* locked up. They were accessible only to the priests and not to
the common people, for it was feared that if anyone could read all
of the *Bible*, even in its altered form, then many more people might
well realise how far removed the practices of the Roman Catholic
Church were from those of Jesus:

Thus, for instance, Fra Fulgentio was reprimanded by the Pope in a letter saying, 'Preaching of the Scriptures is a suspicious thing. He who keeps close to the Scriptures will ruin the Catholic faith.' In his next letter he was more explicit, warning against too much insistence on the Scriptures, 'which is a book if anyone keeps close to, he will quite destroy the Catholic Church.' [4]

The only way the Official Trinitarian Church could maintain its *status quo* was by suppression, repression and oppression.

The fundamental faith of the Catharii, on the other hand, was not conducive to persecution, which was indeed repugnant to it, for acceptance into their number depended upon baptism voluntarily sought for, often with tears and supplication, by a faithful and penitent adult. There could be no dragooning of the unwilling into such a church. On the contrary, the whole purpose of the scrutiny to which a candidate for baptism was subjected, was to ensure that his or her heart and intelligence were won. This was in order to guard against that merely outward show of conformity, which is all that a persecutor can hope to impose.

At the beginning of the thirteenth century, therefore, the Official Roman Catholic Church was in an almost impossible situation. On one hand the institution was threatened with severe corruption from within its own structure. On the other hand it was faced with redundancy on account of the popularity of the teaching of the Unitarian Christian Paulicians. Furthermore, its attention was divided and diverted by its involvement in the folly of the Crusades, for much of its energy and activity at this time was directed towards attempting to halt the rapid advance of Islam and to 'recapture' Jerusalem:

The leaders at the Vatican must have seen the marked similarity between the teachings of Islam and the Unitarianism preached by Arius. Both believed in One God. Both accepted Jesus as a Prophet who, nevertheless, was still a man. Both believed in the Virgin Mary and in the immaculate conception of Jesus. Both accepted the Holy Spirit. Both rejected the divinity which had been attributed to Jesus. It is hardly surprising that the hatred which the Roman Catholic Church had directed at the Unitarian Arians for centuries was now turned against the Muslims as well.

When viewed from this perspective, the mediaeval Crusades – as indeed is also the case with the more modern Crusades being waged in the Balkans today – cease to be an isolated phenomenon of Church history, and become an extension of the massacre of the Arians and the Donatists by the early Pauline Church. [5]

There is no scope in the present work to cover the phenomenon of the Crusades either in depth or detail. They began and ended in confusion, and many people died in the process:

The *First Crusade* which began in 1096 was formed, writes Gibbon, mostly of thieves and criminals. This was the consequence of the Council of Clermont in 1095, in which the Pope proclaimed that anyone who joined the Crusade would be given full dispensation of all his or her sins and would be relieved of any canonical penance he or she might owe. The practice of granting dispensations had been instituted in the fifth century by the Roman Catholic Church. In return for a sum of money the Pope would grant a licence either to excuse or to permit an action which was otherwise canonically illegal. Similarly, anyone who had made use of the rite of confession and had been given a very heavy penance to absolve his or her sins, could pay the Official Church money instead. These practices, none of which were a part of the guidance originally brought by Jesus, peace be on him, helped make the Official Church very rich and many of the people very poor.

As a result of the decree of the Council of Clermont, anyone who had committed some wrong action, ranging from theft to murder, flocked under the banner of the cross. This rabble of some 60,000 men and women pillaged their way across Europe. On reaching Hungary they came face to face with the Paulicians whose forefathers had originally been driven north from Thrace by the persecution of the Empress Theodora and her successors. There was a major battle, and two-thirds of the Crusaders were killed. The survivors took refuge in the mountains of Thrace. The Emperor of Constantinople came to their rescue and safely conducted them to the city. When they reached Constantinople, its treasures proved a great temptation for them, and they may well have plundered the city had not the Emperor swiftly conducted them over the Bosphorus.

Reinforcements of better-trained soldiers were sent to join the remnants of the first Crusaders. When, led by Godfrey, they arrived at Constantinople, they proceeded to fight the Emperor and laid siege to the city. The Emperor, however, managed to bribe and persuade them to hold to their original plan which had been, after all, to fight the Muslims and to take Jerusalem, and they too were conducted across the Bosphorus. Godfrey eventually reached and conquered Jerusalem in 1099.

The *Second Crusade* was undertaken forty-eight years after the fall of Jerusalem, in 1147, in order to support the survivors of the first Crusade whose progress had come to a standstill. It followed much the same pattern as that of the first Crusade. The gates of the cities both in Europe and in Asia were closely barred against the Crusaders, and food was only let down to them from the walls in baskets. This food was of the poorest quality, stale, and often unfit for human consumption. The Crusaders were plagued by famine and pestilence. Many of them died before they reached Palestine. The survivors were killed in battle. Jerusalem was reconquered by the Muslims in 1187.

The *Third Crusade*, led by, among others, King Richard of England, failed to recapture Jerusalem. Richard returned to England in 1192 with the remnants of an army which had been decimated by shipwreck and battle.

The *Fourth Crusade* chose an easier object of conquest and, despite the fact that Constantinople had been in the hands of Trinitarian Christians like themselves for at least three centuries, the Crusaders succeeded where the members of the first two Crusades had failed. In 1203, they burst into the ancient capital of the East, pillaging and plundering in an excess of greed and debauchery. Many of the churches in the capital were ransacked, and the booty taken from them not only subsequently popularised the practice of image-worship in the west, but also greatly increased the wealth of the Roman Catholic Church:

> The most enlightened of the strangers, above the gross and sensual pursuits of their countrymen, more piously exercised the right of conquest in the search and seizure of the relics of the saints. Immense was the supply of heads and bones, crosses and images, that were scattered by this revolution over the churches of Europe;

and such was the increase of pilgrimage and oblation, that no branch, perhaps, of more lucrative plunder was imported from the east. Of the writings of antiquity, many that still existed in the twelfth century are now lost ... without computing the extent of our loss, we may drop a tear over the libraries that have perished in the triple fire of Constantinople. [6]

As has been pointed out by the authors elsewhere, one of the explanations for this dramatic event can probably be traced back to the time of Leo the Iconoclast in the eighth century when, as we have already seen in Chapter Eight, the Churches of Rome and Constantinople split over the issue of image-worship – for even though both Churches subsequently officially agreed to approve the use of images, at the second Council of Nicea in 787, they never re-united:

> This ruling finally resulted, after many years, in the widespread use again of images not only by the Greek Orthodox Church, but also by what became known as the Russian Orthodox Church. By the time that both the Eastern and Western Trinitarian Churches were united once more in this practice of permitting and using images, however, they had drifted so far apart in other respects – especially as regards their respective ruling hierarchies – that it would have been impossible for them ever to re-unite again under a single head of 'the Christian Church'.
>
> It is in the light of this split between the Eastern and the Western Churches that the sack of Constantinople during the fourth Crusade, in 1203 AD, by a Roman Catholic army – which had ostensibly set out to 'liberate' Jerusalem from the Muslims – can be understood. Although the majority of the inhabitants of Constantinople at the time were Trinitarian Christians, and accordingly subscribed to the same basic religious doctrines as the majority of the members of the army which was attacking them, the two 'sides' were nevertheless far enough apart ideologically for one to be able to regard the other as 'the enemy'. [7]

Despite the wealth which accrued from the sack of Constantinople, the Crusades were a costly business, not only financially but in terms of lives. With the growth of the Paulician movement in France, the Roman Catholic Church was forced to direct its attention towards securing its position in Europe itself. This change in emphasis was probably one of the major reasons for the failure of the *Fifth Crusade*, which started in 1218. The Official Roman Catholic Church had by then committed itself to attacking the Muslims of Sicily and North Africa, the Muslims of Turkey and Palestine, the Muslims of Spain, and now the Paulician Catharii of France. It was impossible to maintain a successful degree of aggression on all fronts at all four points of the compass for very long. Inevitably the Church was forced to reduce its ambitious activities, and to direct its attention towards its enemies who were nearest Rome.

❍   ❍   ❍   ❍   ❍

The persecution of the Paulician Catharii in France began in earnest at the very beginning of the thirteenth century. As we have seen, it was directed at those Unitarian Christians who were settled in Albigeois, which is why they are often referred to as the Albigenses.

A papal legate called Peter was assassinated in the south of France in 1208, and the Albigenses were held responsible. Pope Innocent III called for a crusade to be directed against them. Simon de Montfort was chosen to lead it. The massacre of Beziers was perhaps his most notable victory. Reginald, the Bishop of Beziers, was with the crusading forces, and when they arrived before the city he obtained from the legate authority to offer the town full exemption if the heretics, of whom he had a list, were delivered up to him.

When he entered the town, and called its chief inhabitants together, the offer was unanimously spurned. Since most of the families in the town had at least some Unitarian Christian members, they were not willing to expose their own relations and friends to the torture and death, which anyone handed over to the papal legate would face:

> Catharians and Catholics were too firmly united in bonds of common relationship and old associations for one to betray the other ... This unexpected answer stirred the legate to such wrath that he swore to destroy

the place with fire and sword ... The legate's oath was fulfilled by a massacre almost without parallel in European history. From infancy in arms to tottering age, not one was spared – seven thousand, it is said, were slaughtered in the Church of Mary Magdalen to which they had fled for asylum – and the total number of slain is set down by the legates at nearly twenty thousand. [8]

Since the population of Beziers at that time was at least one hundred thousand people, it is likely that the number of slain was much higher than the official record, for:

When Arnaud was asked whether the Catholics should be spared, he feared the heretics would escape by feigning orthodoxy, and fiercely replied, 'Kill them all, for God knows his own.' [9]

This massacre, whose details writers of European history often choose to omit, together with the Battle of Murat in 1213 in which Simon de Montfort won a decisive victory over the Unitarian Christians, signalled the beginning of another intense burst of activity by the Official Trinitarian Church against the Paulicians. The Mediaeval version of the Inquisition was launched into action and it mercilessly persecuted the 'heretics' and burnt both them and their books. Like the other Unitarian Christians of the past, there is hardly any record left today of the Paulician Catharii. They and their books have been virtually wiped out.

◯   ◯   ◯   ◯   ◯

It is often claimed in retrospect, by a somewhat embarrassed Official Roman Catholic Church, that the Mediaeval Inquisition was not initiated specifically to exterminate those who affirmed the Divine Unity. It is said that initially this institution was more concerned with reconditioning corrupt priests and converting people to the religion of the Catholic Church. This view is supported by the words of Pope Innocent III who, in his opening address to the great Lateran Council in 1215, declared:

The corruption of the people has its chief source in the clergy. From this arise the evils of Christendom: faith perishes, religion is defaced, liberty is restricted, justice is trodden underfoot, the 'heretics' multiply, the 'schismatics' are emboldened, the faithless grow strong, the Saracens are victorious. [10]

As the Mediaeval Inquisition evolved, however, it soon directed its activities away from the curing of its own corruption, and turned its attention towards the elimination of 'heretics'. The success of the Mediaeval Inquisition in this field was largely due to two factors: Its functions were supported by extensive laws, and they were carried out by able administrators. All the ecclesiastical bulls and canons, especially those of Pope Innocent II, were incorporated into the secular law of Italy and France. The work of capturing 'heretics', and extorting their confessions before handing them over to the secular authorities for punishment, was performed by the mendicant orders of the Franciscans and the Dominicans, and before examining the activities of the Mediaeval Inquisition in greater detail, it would be illuminating to make a brief study of the origins and destiny of these two brotherhoods.

◉   ◉   ◉   ◉   ◉

The two great orders of the Franciscans and the Dominicans grew out of an attempt to return to a simple life of poverty based on the life of Jesus, peace be on him, as related in the official gospels. Both of their leaders, Francis and Dominic, received papal recognition at the beginning of the thirteenth century, when their respective followings were still very small. The two brotherhoods grew very rapidly, since the first members provided a far healthier and more honest example and source of guidance than the corrupt priests of the Official Roman Catholic Church.

Their two movements, however, were quite distinct and separate from those of the Waldenses and the Paulician Catharii. Although they had begun in an attempt to regain a way of life closer to that of Jesus, the Franciscans and the Dominicans never affirmed the Divine Unity, but rather believed in the Trinitarian dogma of the Official Church. They were thus a regenerative energy within the structure of the Official Church and not apart from it. Since these brotherhoods were based on a high standard of discipline and obedience, both amongst themselves and to the Pope, they soon proved themselves to be invaluable agents for the head of the Official Roman Catholic Church:

Their peculiar devotion to the Holy See rendered them specially useful in organising the papal Inquisition which was to supersede by degrees the episcopal jurisdiction, and prove so efficient an instrument in reducing the local churches to subjection. [11]

The Mediaeval version of the Inquisition has sometimes been said to have been founded on April 20, 1233, the day on which Pope Gregory issued two papal bulls making the persecution of 'heresy' the special function of the Dominicans. The first bull was addressed to the clergy of the Roman Catholic Church. After reciting the necessity of subduing 'heresy', and discussing the raising up by God of the preaching friars, 'who devote themselves in voluntary poverty to spreading the Word and extirpating misbelief', Pope Gregory proceeded to tell the bishops:

> We, seeing you engrossed in the whirlwind of cares and scarce able to breathe in the pressure of overwhelming anxieties, think it well to divide your burdens that they may be more easily borne. We have therefore determined to send preaching friars against the 'heretics' of France and the adjoining provinces, and we beg, warn and exhort you, ordering you, as you reverence the Holy See, to receive them kindly and treat them well, giving them in this, as in all else, favour, counsel and aid, that they may fulfil their office. [12]

The second bull was addressed to 'the Priors, and Friars of the Order of Preachers, Inquisitors', and after alluding to the 'sons of perdition' who defend 'heresy', it proceeds:

> Therefore you, or any of you, wherever you may happen to preach, are empowered, unless they desist from such defence (of 'heretics') or monition, to deprive clerks of their benefices forever, and to proceed against them and all others, without appeal, calling in the aid of the secular arm, if necessary, and coercing opposition if requisite, with the censures of the Church, without appeal. [13]

When the Dominican Friars arrived in France, they were not welcomed by the priesthood of the Official Trinitarian Church; for hav-

ing found popularity with many people, the Friars began to perform all the functions which the old priesthood had relied on as
their main source of income. A concerted effort was made to have
the privileges of the Orders removed, but it failed. A petition was
made to Clement VI for the abolition of the Orders, or at least the
prohibition of their preaching and hearing confessions, and enjoy-
ing the burial profits by which, especially during the time of the
plague, they were enormously enriched at the expense of the par-
ish priests. Pope Clement VI, however, denied the main allegation
of the petition that the Friars were useless to the Roman Catholic
Church, and he asserted that, on the contrary, they were most valu-
able:

> 'And if,' he continued, 'their preaching be stopped,
> about what can you preach to the people? If on humil-
> ity, you your selves are the proudest of the world, arro-
> gant and given to pomp. If on poverty, you are the most
> grasping and most covetous, so that all the benefices in
> the world will not satisfy you. If on chastity – but we
> will be silent on this, for God knoweth what each man
> does and how many of you satisfy your lusts. You hate
> the Mendicants and shut your doors on them lest they
> should see your mode of life, while you waste your tem-
> poral wealth on pimps and swindlers. You should not
> complain if the Mendicants receive some temporal pos-
> sessions from the dying to whom they minister when
> you have fled, nor that they spend it in buildings where
> everything is ordered for the honour of God and the
> Church, in place of wasting it in pleasure and licentious-
> ness. And because you do not likewise, you accuse the
> Mendicants, for most of you give yourselves up to vain
> and worldly lives.' [14]

The Friars continued their work in France and their numbers increased. By now the Franciscan Friars were as numerous in France
as the Dominicans. Having established their presence in the country, they turned to the elimination of heretics. As conversion became less the object, and persecution the main business, of the Inquisition, the Franciscans became equally as useful as the Dominicans, and the honours of the institution were divided between them.
The two brotherhoods formed an efficient, mobile and widespread
organisation. They became the perfect instrument of the Pope to

eliminate 'heresy'. Once established they became very rich and very powerful, and eventually suffered the same degeneration and corruption as the old Official Trinitarian Church, to which they had originally grown up in opposition. The original visions and precepts of their founders were forgotten. Those who tried to keep to them were ridiculed.

St. Francis himself had foretold on his deathbed, as he lay naked beneath a blanket, possessing nothing, that his Order would become so defamed that it would be ashamed to be seen in public. Lea writes:

> As the Order spread it was not in human nature to reject the wealth which came pouring in upon it from all sides, and ingenious dialectics were resorted to, to reconcile its ample possessions with the absolute rejection of property prescribed by the Rule. The humble hovels which Francis had enjoined became stately palaces which arose in every city, rivalling or putting to shame the loftiest cathedrals and most sumptuous abbeys. [15]

Birgitta, in her *Revelations*, which were sanctioned by the Official Roman Catholic Church as being 'inspired' declares that:

> Although founded upon vows of poverty, they have amassed riches, place their whole aim in increasing their wealth, dress as richly as bishops, and many of them are more extravagant in their jewellery and ornaments than laymen who are reputed wealthy. [16]

When Pope John XXII eventually stigmatised as 'heretical' the belief that Christ had lived in absolute poverty, he thereby transformed the last of the Friars who might still be following the founders of their brotherhoods into unpardonable criminals whom the temporal officials were bound to send to the stake, under pain of being themselves treated as 'heretics' if they did not. By the year 1519 Erasmus was complaining in a letter to Albert, Cardinal-Archbishop of Mainz:

> The world is overburdened with the tyranny of the Mendicants, who, though they are the satellites of the Roman See, are yet so numerous and powerful that they

are formidable to the Pope himself and even to kings. To them, when the Pope aids them, he is more than God, when he displeases them he is worthless as a dream. [17]

It was to these rich and powerful brotherhoods that the duties of Inquisitors were entrusted, and once the Mediaeval Inquisition in France was established, they became a law unto themselves.

○   ○   ○   ○   ○

The process by which the designs of the Official Church became the law of the land was a rapid one. At the Lateran Council of 1215, Innocent III instituted a series of severe regulations defining the attitude of the Official Roman Catholic Church towards 'heretics', and the duties which the secular power owed to exterminate them. These regulations became a recognised part of canon law but were not immediately incorporated into the secular law.

This disparity in the two branches of the law was soon remedied by Frederic II, who had to win the favour of Pope Honorius III in order to secure his coronation. This took place in 1220, on the understanding that Frederic II would then make the persecution of 'heretics' legal. In a series of edicts dating from 1220 to 1239 he thus enacted a complete and pitiless code of persecution, based upon the Lateran canons:

Those who were merely suspected of heresy were required to purge themselves at the command of the Roman Catholic Church, under penalty of being deprived of civil rights and placed under the imperial ban; while, if they remained in this condition for a year, they were to be condemned as heretics. 'Heretics' of all sects were outlawed; and when condemned as such by the Official Church they were to be delivered to the secular arm to be burned. If, through fear of death, they recanted, they were to be thrust in prison for life there to perform penance. If they relapsed into 'error' thus showing that their conversion had been fictitious, they were to be put to death. All the property of the heretic was confiscated and his heirs disinherited. His children to the second generation were declared ineligible to any positions of emolument or dignity, unless they should win mercy by betraying their father or some other heretic. All those who helped or defended heretics in any way were banished forever, their property confiscated, and their descendants subjected to the same disabilities as those of heretics.

Those who defended the errors of heretics were to be treated as heretics unless, on admonition, they mended their ways. The houses of the heretics and their receivers were to be destroyed never to be rebuilt. Although the evidence of a heretic was not receivable in court, yet an exception was made in favour of the faith, and it was held good against another heretic. All rulers and magistrates, present or future, were required to swear to exterminate with their utmost ability all whom the Official Church might designate as heretics, under pain of forfeiture of office.

When the papal Inquisition was officially inaugurated and put in the charge of the friars, Frederic II hastened, in 1232, to place the whole machinery of the state at the command of the inquisitors, who were authorised to call upon any official to capture whomsoever they might designate as a 'heretic', and hold him in prison until the Roman Catholic Church should condemn him, when he was to be put to death. [18]

The decrees made by Frederic II were strengthened by the Council of Narbonne in 1244. An even more elaborate series of canons were framed, which remained the basis of inquisitorial action, and which ensured the full co-operation of the secular authorities. Anyone holding temporal jurisdiction who delayed in exterminating heretics was held guilty of fautorship of heresy, becoming an accomplice of heretics, and thus was subjected to the penalties of heresy. This was extended to all who should neglect a favourable opportunity of capturing a heretic, or of helping those seeking to capture him. Everyone in the land was thus compelled by fear of death to help implement Official Church policy:

> From the emperor to the meanest peasant the duty of persecution was enforced with all the sanctions, spiritual and temporal, which the Church could command. Not only must the ruler enact rigorous laws to punish 'heretics', but he and his subjects must see them strenuously executed, for any slackness of persecution was, in the canon law, construed as fautorship of heresy, putting a man on his purgation.
>
> These principles were tacitly or explicitly received into the public law of Europe ... The inquisitor was commanded to coerce all officials to their rigid enforcement, by excommunicating those who were negligent in the

'good work'. Even excommunication, which rendered a magistrate incompetent to perform his official functions, did not relieve him from the duty of punishing 'heretics' when called upon by bishop or inquisitor. [19]

The measures governing the jurisdiction and functions of the Mediaeval Inquisition culminated in and were basically completed by the famous bull, '*Ad Extirpanda*' – 'Towards Obliteration', which was issued by Pope Innocent IV to all the potentates and governors of Italy, on May 15, 1252. This carefully considered and elaborate law established the machinery for systematic persecution as an integral part of the social edifice in every city and every state, and it was soon adopted in France as well. It ordered and standardised the various offices within the Inquisition, giving them almost unlimited freedom of action. Their sole business was to arrest 'heretics', seize their property, and deliver them to the bishop, or his vicars, who would pronounce the victim's spiritual guilt, before passing him over to the local authorities to be burnt.

The Inquisitors' wages and expenses were to be defrayed by the state, their evidence was receivable without oaths, and no testimony was good against the concurrent statement of any three of them. They were entitled to one third of the proceeds of all fines and confiscations inflicted on 'heretics', which partly explains how the friars became so rich so swiftly. They were exempt from all public duties and services incompatible with their functions, and no statutes were to be passed interfering with their actions.

The governors and officials of any province or potentate were bound to help the Inquisitors whenever they visited them, and every inhabitant when called upon to do so was obliged to assist them, under a heavy penalty if he or she did not. When the Inquisitors visited any district within their jurisdiction, they were accompanied by a deputy of the local governor elected by themselves or by the bishop. In each place visited, this official was to summon under oath three men of good repute, or even the whole vicarage if necessary, to reveal any 'heretics' within their knowledge, or the property of such, or of anyone holding secret gatherings or differing in life or manners from the 'ordinary' Christians. These methods, used by the Inquisitors to winkle out 'heretics' when they came to a village or a town for the first time, were to be perfected by the Spanish Inquisition who, as we shall see in *Islam in Andalus, insh'Allah*, introduced the notorious 'Edict of Grace' and then subsequently the 'Edict of Faith' in order to render these measures more efficient

The local authorities were bound to arrest all those who were accused of 'heresy', to hold them in prison, to deliver them to the bishop or Inquisitor under safe escort, and to execute within fifteen days, in accordance with Frederic II's decrees, all judgements pronounced against them. The governor was further required, when called upon, to inflict torture on those who would not confess and betray all the heretics of their acquaintance. If resistance was made to an arrest, the whole community where this occurred was liable to an enormous fine unless it delivered up to justice within three days all who were implicated. The proceeds of fines, commutations and confiscations were divisible into three parts: one was given to the city, one to those concerned in the business, and the remainder to the bishop and Inquisitors to be expended in persecuting heresy.

The enforcement of these draconian measures contained in the bull of Pope Innocent IV was provided for with equally careful elaboration. They were to be inscribed ineffaceably in all the local statute-books, together with all subsequent laws which the Popes might issue, under penalty of excommunication for recalcitrant officials, and interdict upon the city. Any attempt to alter these laws consigned the offender to perpetual infamy and fine, enforced by the ban. The governors and their officials were to swear to their observance under pain of loss of office. Any neglect in their enforcement was punishable as perjury with perpetual infamy, a fine of two hundred marks, and suspicion of heresy – which involved loss of office, disability for all official positions in the future, and the likelihood of being tortured and killed as a heretic.

Every governor, within ten days after assuming office, was required to investigate the acts of his predecessor and prosecute him for any failure of obedience. Every governor at the beginning and end of his term was required to have the bull read out in all places that might be designated by the bishop and the Inquisitors, and to erase from the statute-books all laws in conflict with them. At the same time Pope Innocent IV issued instructions to the Inquisitors to enforce by excommunication the embodiment of this bull, and of the edicts of King Frederic II, in the statutes of all cities and states. He soon after conferred on them the dangerous power of interpreting, in conjunction with the bishops, all doubtful points in local laws on the subject of heresy.

These laws, combined with the efficiency of the Friars in implementing and enforcing them, made the Mediaeval Inquisition a formidable means of destruction. Its activities were surpassed only by the Spanish Inquisition which grew from it, and which may be regarded as a continuation of it. They provide perhaps the most elaborate and detailed example of an attempt to enforce the religion of the Official Church in its entire history. In Lea's words:

> These provisions are not the wild imaginings of a nightmare, but sober matter-of-fact legislation shrewdly and carefully devised to accomplish a settled policy, and it affords us a valuable insight into the public opinion of the day to find that there was no effective resistance to its acceptance. [20]

In the exercise of this almost limitless authority, the Inquisitors were relieved from practically all supervision and responsibility. They were not liable to excommunication while in discharge of their duties, nor could they be suspended by any delegate of the Holy See. Commissions were continually issued directly by the Pope, and those who held them seem not to have been removable by anyone else except him. They acknowledged responsibility only to the Pope. Their jurisdiction was thus almost unlimited, for suspicion of heresy was to be technically inferred from anything which affected the dignity or crossed the purpose of those who carried out the work of the Inquisition. Thus anyone who opposed the Inquisitors soon ended up 'lawfully' dead:

> That laymen learned to address them as 'your religious majesty' shows the impression made on the popular mind by their irresponsible supremacy ... It required, indeed, courage to foolhardiness for anyone to raise hand or voice against an Inquisitor, no matter how cruel or nefarious were his actions. Under canon law, anyone, from the meanest to the highest, who opposed or impeded in any way the functions of an Inquisitor, or gave aid or counsel to those who did so, became at once *ipso facto* excommunicate. After the lapse of a year in this condition he was legally a heretic to be handed over without further ceremony to the secular arm for burning, without trial and without forgiveness. The awful au-

thority which thus shrouded the Inquisitor was rendered yet more terrible by the elasticity of definition given to the crime of impeding the Holy Office and the tireless tenacity with which those guilty of it were pursued. [21]

The fear which the Inquisitors instilled in people's hearts was perhaps their greatest weapon in detecting 'heretics', although it must have often driven people to tell lies rather than the truth. The Inquisitors were faced with the impossible task of ascertaining the secret thoughts and opinions of their prisoners, and their methods were calculated to simplify the process by putting the words they wanted to hear into the mouths of their victims:

The first thing demanded of the offender when he or she appeared before the tribunal was an oath to stand to the mandates of the Roman Catholic Church, to answer truly all questions asked of him or her, to betray all heretics known to him or her, and to perform whatever penance might be imposed on him or her. Refusal to take this oath was to proclaim oneself at once a defiant and obstinate heretic, but even if he or she agreed to give the oath, it was still necessary to convince the Inquisitors that he or she was speaking the truth:

> That plain-spoken friar, Bernard Délicieux, uttered the literal truth when he declared, in the presence of Philippe le Bel and all his court that if St. Peter and St. Paul were accused of 'adoring' heretics and were prosecuted after the fashion of the Inquisition, there would be no defence open for them. Questioned as to their faith, they would answer like masters in theology and doctors of the Church, but when told that they had adored heretics, and they asked what heretics, some names common in those parts, would be mentioned, but no particulars would be given. When they would ask for statements as to time and place, no facts would be furnished, and when they would demand the names of the witnesses, these would be withheld. How, then, asked Bernard, could the holy apostles defend themselves, especially when anyone who wished to aid them would himself be attacked as a fautor of heresy? It was so. The victim was enveloped in a net from which there was no escape, and his frantic struggles only twisted it more tightly around him. [22]

The Mediaeval Inquisitors usually resorted to torture, which was common in judicial practice throughout Europe at this time, in order to ensure that they were obtaining the right answers. Some of the tortures which they used derived from those which had been used against the Arians and the Donatists in North Africa under the Theodosian Code. As well as what took place in secret, the accused persons were often publicly subjected to '*Judicium Dei*', the 'Judgement of God', in the Trials by Water and Fire. These physical tests, which originated from the practices of the Franks, and which were popular in Europe from about 450 AD onwards, were sanctioned by the Official Roman Catholic Church, even though they are not mentioned in the *Bible*, and were conducted under the direction of its clergy. The outcome was regarded as the immediate judgment of God, for it was expected that fire should not burn the innocent, and that the pure element of water would not allow the guilty to sink into its midst.

The most popular of these tests was the Hot Iron Test, in which the accused carried a ball of red-hot iron in his hand for nine steps. If burnt, he was guilty. In the Plough Share Test the accused was told to walk blindfold between two red-hot plough-shares. If burnt by them, he was guilty. In the Hot Water Test, the accused was told to plunge his arm into a cauldron of boiling water, either up to the wrist or to the elbow according to the gravity of the charge. The scalded part of his arm was then bandaged. After three days had elapsed, the priest examined it. If the scald was not healed, he was guilty. In the Cold Water Test the accused was tied up and thrown into deep water. If he floated – and anyone who takes a deep breath before plunging into water usually does – he was guilty. If he sank he was innocent, but if, because he was unable to swim, he drowned, then this was taken as proof of his guilt. Perhaps the most lenient of these tests was the Dry Bread Test, in which the accused was given an ounce of dry bread or cheese to swallow. If it stuck in his throat, he was guilty. Since one of the effects of fear is a dry throat, only the fearless could pass this test. These trials by ordeal were always preceded by an Official Church mass. The Council of Rheims in 1157 decreed that Trial by Ordeal should be used in all cases of suspected heresy.

In prosecutions for heresy the ecclesiastical tribunal passed no judgments of blood. It merely found the defendant to be a heretic. Once the guilt of a heretic was established, the Inquisitors then handed him over to the secular authorities with the hypocritical adjuration to be merciful to him, to spare his life and not to spill his blood. The authorities were then bound to burn, or at least imprison for life, their victim, under the threat of themselves being punished as heretics if they did not. This sophisticated but transparently unjust procedure was no less than an attempt to absolve all parties concerned from being responsible for their own actions:

> The penal functions of the Inquisition were based on a fiction which must be comprehended in order rightly to appreciate much of its action. Theoretically it had no power to inflict punishment. Its mission was to save men's souls ... Its sentences, therefore, were not like those of an earthly judge, the retaliation of society on the wrong-doer, or deterrent examples to prevent the spread of crime; they were simply imposed for the benefit of the erring soul, to wash away its sin. [23]

This paternalistic and supposedly philanthropic argument, however, was no less than an attempt to hide the fact that the distinction made between the 'secular' authorities and the 'ecclesiastical' authorities, was entirely imaginary. The two institutions were in reality the same body whose motivating force was from within that body. The Official Church was establishing its religion in the only way possible to do so, by force. And the action of the secular authority was in no way separate from, but indeed was an expression and an extension of, the motivating force of the Official Church:

> The continuous teachings of the Church led its best men to regard no act as more self-evidently just than the burning of the 'heretic', and no 'heresy' less defensible than a demand for toleration ... The fact is, the Church not only defined the guilt and forced its punishment, but created the crime itself. [24]

        ❂   ❂   ❂   ❂   ❂

The whole terrible might of the Mediaeval Inquisition was directed against the Paulician Catharii during the thirteenth and fourteenth centuries, and not only those who affirmed and worshipped the Divine Unity and denied the dogma of Trinitarianism, but also anyone who refused to practise the official religion was mercilessly hounded down and killed.

The fact that suspicion of heresy was reason enough to arrest and torture a person, gave the Inquisitors a wide latitude in selecting their victims and, if necessary, it could be used to eliminate anyone – even orthodox Trinitarians – whom the Inquisitors wished to remove. However there was no difficulty in detecting the true Paulicians, for they were easily recognisable by the Inquisitors because of the way in which they behaved. An Inquisitor who knew them well described them in these words:

> Heretics are recognisable by their customs and speech, for they are modest and well regulated. They take no pride in their garments, which are neither costly nor vile. They do not engage in trade, to avoid lies and oaths and frauds, but they live by their labour as mechanics – their teachers are cobblers. They do not accumulate wealth, but are content with necessaries. They are chaste and temperate in meat and drink. They do not frequent taverns or dances or other vanities. They restrain themselves from anger. They are always at work; they teach and learn and consequently pray but little. They are to be known by their modesty and precision of speech, avoiding scurrility and detraction and light words and lies and oaths. [25]

It is clear that their only crime was the affirmation and worship of the Divine Unity and their rejection of the doctrine of Trinity, for:

> As St. Bernard says, 'If you interrogate them, nothing can be more Christian; as to their conversation, nothing can be less reprehensible, and what they speak they prove by deeds. As for the morals of the heretic, he cheats no-one, he oppresses no-one, he strikes no-one; his cheeks are pale with fasting, he eats not the bread of idleness, his hands labour for his livelihood. [26]

Even in the face of death, the Paulician Catharii retained their honesty and sincerity:

> It was the general testimony that the perfected heretic refused to lie, or to take an oath; and one member of the Holy Office warns his brethren not to begin by asking,

'Are you truly a Cathari?' for the answer will simply be 'Yes', and then nothing more can be extracted; but if the perfect is exhorted by the God in whom he believes to tell all about his life, he will faithfully detail it without falsehood. When we consider that this frankness led inevitably to the torture of death by burning, it is curious to observe that the Inquisitor seems utterly unconscious of the emphatic testimony which he renders to the super-human conscientiousness of his victims. [27]

It is impossible to estimate how many Unitarian Christians were eliminated by the Mediaeval Inquisition in the name of the Official Trinitarian Church, and 'for Christ's sake'. The *'Liber Sententiarum'*, which is the record of the Inquisition of Toulouse from 1307 to 1323, after a century of merciless persecution, alone has 400 closely written folio pages which barely suffice to chronicle the cruelties perpetuated in the Name of the God of Mercy, by the clergy of the 'orthodox' Catholic Church of Rome. Conybeare writes:

A hundred such volumes would be needed to record the whole tale of suppression of the European Cathariis. [28]

The success of the Mediaeval Inquisition can be measured by the fact that there is no trace of the Paulician movement alive in Europe today. Like the Arian Goths before them, the Paulician Catharii, their books and their teaching, in its totality, have disappeared off the face of the earth.

    ⊙   ⊙   ⊙   ⊙   ⊙

Unlike the Paulician Catharii, the influence of the Mediaeval Inquisition continued for several centuries. The activities of the Inquisitors pervaded the whole fabric of society to such a degree that traces of their ideology are still present within the legal systems of the Continent of Europe today. The use of torture and the inquisitorial process were almost exclusively adopted in all European judicial processes, and the fact that they became the prominent characteristic of the criminal jurisprudence of Europe may solely be ascribed to the fact that they received the sanction of the Official Roman Catholic Church. Thus recommended, they penetrated everywhere along with the Inquisition:

Of all the curses which the Inquisition brought in its train this, perhaps, was the greatest – that, until the closing years of the eighteenth century throughout the greater part of Europe, the inquisitorial process, as developed for the destruction of 'heresy', became the customary method of dealing with all who were under accusation; that the accused was treated as one having no rights, whose guilt was assumed in advance, and from whom confession was to be extorted by guile or force. Even witnesses were treated in the same fashion; and the prisoner who acknowledged guilt under torture was tortured again to obtain information about any other evildoers of whom he perchance might have knowledge. So, also, the crime of 'suspicion' was imported from the Inquisition into ordinary practice, and the accused who could not be convicted of the crime laid to his door could be punished for being suspected of it, not with the penalty legally provided for the offence, but with some other, at the fancy and discretion of the judge.

Lea continues:

It would be impossible to compute the amount of misery and wrong, inflicted on the defenceless up to the present century, which may be directly traced to the arbitrary and unrestricted methods introduced by the Inquisition and adopted by the jurists who fashioned the criminal jurisprudence of the Continent. It was a system which might well seem the invention of demons, and was fitly characterised by Sir John Fortescue as the Road to Hell. [29]

And even today, when the days of the Mediaeval Inquisition are long passed, and when relatively few people even know that it once existed, or can even begin to understand the tortuous reasoning that was used to justify the atrocities that it perpetrated in the Name of God, for Christ's sake, or are even vaguely aware of how many Unitarian Christians were prepared to die, for Christ's sake, English legal textbooks still refer, by way of comparison with the English legal system, for example, to the 'inquisitorial process' which is followed in France.

o   o   o   o   o

Postface

Having traced the movements of the Nazarenes, the Donatists, the Arians, and the Paulicians, from beginning to end, and having analysed the sustained persecution of these Unitarian Christians by the Official Trinitarian Church which grew up in opposition to them, it is now possible to examine and understand the extraordinary flowering and then the almost complete destruction of Islam in Andalus, as the Iberian peninsula is called in Arabic – for the story of the virtual genocide of all the Muslims in Spain and Portugal (today it would be euphemistically described as 'ethnic cleansing') is intimately linked with that of the Paulician Unitarian Christians:

As we have already seen in Chapter Eight, the Official Roman Catholic Church equated the way of the Paulicians with that of Islam, and accordingly its opposition to these two groups who affirmed the Divine Unity, was regarded as one and the same fight.

It was the supremacy of the Official Roman Catholic Church in the south of France during the thirteenth century – which, as we have just seen was achieved largely as a result of the efforts of the Mediaeval Inquisition in wiping out the Paulician Catharii – that made the north of Spain easily accessible to the Christian armies, which, although at one time divided against each other, were united by Pope Innocent III in their attempts to eliminate Islam in Spain.

Thus it does not really come as a surprise to learn that the methods of persecution used by the Mediaeval Inquisition against the Paulician Catharii were developed and perfected by its successor, the Spanish Inquisition. These techniques of destruction were used with devastating results not only against the Muslims, but also against the Jews and the last of the Unitarian Christians, both in Spain and in Portugal.

The actions of the Spanish Inquisition in the Iberian peninsula, as we shall see, *insh'Allah*, in *Islam in Andalus*, followed the same pattern of behaviour as had been displayed by the Trinitarian Church ever since its inception – and especially in the times of Constantine, and Theodosius, and Justinian, and Theodora – towards those who rejected the Paulinian version of Christianity and who, following in the footsteps of Jesus and his true followers, peace be on him and them, affirmed and worshipped the Divine Unity.

o   o   o   o   o

Chapter Notes

Introduction

1. V. Robinson, *The Story of Medicine*, p. 164.

Chapter One: The Nazarenes and the Christians

1. M. Ata'ur-Rahim and A. Thomson, *Jesus Prophet of Islam – Revised Edition*, p. 35.
2. *The Gospel of Barnabas*: 217.
3. *The Gospel of Barnabas*: 218.
4. Cross, *The Oxford Dictionary of Christianity*, p. 274.
5. St. Augustine, *De Civitate Dei*, 10.23.
6. E. Gibbon, *Decline and Fall of the Roman Empire*, II, p. 9.
7. Le Clerc, *The Apostolic Fathers*, p. 84.
8. E. Gibbon, *Decline and Fall of the Roman Empire*, II, p. 12.
9. Ibid, IV, p. 418.
10. Ibid, IV, p. 418.
11. Ibid, VI, p. 10.
12. Ibid, VI, p. 55.
13. Ibid, VI, p. 10.
14. M. Ata'ur-Rahim and A. Thomson, *Jesus Prophet of Islam – Revised Edition*, p. 73.
15. E. Gibbon, *Decline and Fall of the Roman Empire*, II, p. 119.
16. Ibid, II, p. 120.
17. Ibid, II, p. 120.
18. Ibid, II, p. 216.
19. M. Ata'ur-Rahim and A. Thomson, *Jesus Prophet of Islam – Revised Edition*, p. 73.
20. Ibid, p. 74.
21. E. Gibbon, *Decline and Fall of the Roman Empire*, II, p. 159.
22. Ibid, II, p. 216.
23. Ibid, II, p. 188.

24. Ibid, II, p. 119.
25. M. Ata'ur-Rahim and A. Thomson, *Jesus Prophet of Islam – Revised Edition*, p. 74.

Chapter Two: The Donatists and the Arians

1. E. Gibbon, *Decline and Fall of the Roman Empire*, II, p. 454.
2. Ibid, II, p. 450.
3. Ibid, II, p. 448.
4. Ibid, II, p. 447.
5. Ibid, II, p. 458.
6. Ibid, II, p. 473.
7. Ibid, II, p. 475.
8. Ibid, II, p. 481.
9. Ibid, II, p. 469.
10. M. Ata'ur-Rahim and A. Thomson, *Jesus Prophet of Islam – Revised Edition*, p. 85.
11. Ibid, p. 87.
12. Ibid, p. 91.
13. Ibid, pp. 94-95.
14. Ibid, p. 103.
15. D. Potter, *Sunday Times Weekly Review*, 10th April 1977, p. 1.
16. E. Gibbon, *Decline and Fall of the Roman Empire*, III, p. 23.
17. Ibid, III, p. 399.
18. Ibid, III, p. 400.
19. Ibid, III, p. 408.
20. Ibid, III, p. 412.
21. Ibid, III, p. 413.
22. Ibid, III, p. 415.
23. Ibid, III, p. 415.
24. T. Hodgkin, *Italy and her Invaders*, p. 440.
25. E. Gibbon, *Decline and Fall of the Roman Empire*, III, p. 440.
26. Ibid, III, p. 440.
27. Ibid, VI, p. 206.
28. Ibid, VI, p. 207.
29. Ibid, VI, p. 216.
30. Ibid, VI, p. 208.

Chapter Three: The Visigoths

1. E. Gibbon, *Decline and Fall of the Roman Empire*, IV, p. 409.
2. Ibid, IV, p. 409.
3. E. Hodgkin, *Italy and her Invaders*, I, p. 256.
4. Ibid, III, p. 406.
5. Ibid, III, p. 406.
6. Ibid, VI, p. 19.
7. C.A.A. Scott, *Ulfilas, Apostle of the Goths*, p. 113.
8. Ibid, p. 115.
9. Ibid, p. 121.
10. Ibid, p. 35.
11. E. Gibbon, *Decline and Fall of the Roman Empire*, III, p. 408.
12. C.A.A. Scott, *Ulfilas, Apostle of the Goths*, p. 167.
13. E. Gibbon, *Decline and Fall of the Roman Empire*, IV, p. 266.
14. Ibid, IV, p. 301.
15. R. Dozy, *Spanish Islam*, p. 23.
16. C.A.A. Scott, *Ulfilas, Apostle of the Goths*.
17. R. Dozy, *Spanish Islam*, p. 223.

Chapter Four: The Vandals

1. E. Gibbon, *Decline and Fall of the Roman Empire*, IV, p. 224.
2. Ibid, IV, p. 220.
3. Ibid, IV, p. 224.
4. Ibid, IV, p. 225.
5. Ibid, IV, p. 228.
6. Ibid, IV, p. 412.
7. Ibid, IV, p. 414.
8. Ibid, IV, p. 417.
9. Ibid, IV, p. 419.
10. Ibid, VI, p. 45.
11. Ibid, VI, p. 48.
12. M. Ata'ur-Rahim and A. Thomson, *Jesus Prophet of Islam – Revised Edition*, p. 89.

Chapter Five: The Ostrogoths

1. C.A.A. Scott, *Ulfilas, Apostle of the Goths*, p. 135.
2. E. Gibbon, *Decline and Fall of the Roman Empire*, IV, p. 378.
3. Ibid, V, p. 15.
4. C.A.A. Scott, *Ulfilas, Apostle of the Goths*, p. 169.
5. E. Gibbon, *Decline and Fall of the Roman Empire*, V, p. 26.
6. Ibid, V, p. 31.
7. Ibid, IV, p. 380.
8. Ibid, IV, p. 438.
9. Ibid, IV, p. 439.
10. Ibid, V, p. 162.

Chapter Six: The Goths in the Iberian Peninsula

1. Castro, *The Structure of Spanish History*, p. 65.
2. Ibid, p. 64.
3. Ibid, p. 62.
4. Ibid, p. 64.
5. Ibid, p. 64.
6. R. Dozy, *Spanish Islam*, p. 222.
7. Ibid, p. 225.
8. C. Kingsley, *Hypathia*, Preface, p. 14.

Chapter Seven: The Jews in the Iberian Peninsula

1. A. Thomson, *The Next World Order*, p. 34.
2. R. Dozy, *Spanish Islam*, p. 231.
3. E. Gibbon, *Decline and Fall of the Roman Empire*, IV, p. 426.
4. Ibid, IV, p. 426.

Chapter Eight: The Early Paulicians

1. F.C. Conybeare, *The Key of Truth*, Preface, p. 12.
2. E. Gibbon, *Decline and Fall of the Roman Empire*, VII, p. 59.
3. F.C. Conybeare, *The Key of Truth*, Preface, p. iii.

4. E. Gibbon, *Decline and Fall of the Roman Empire*, VII, p. 57.

5. M. Ata'ur-Rahim and A. Thomson, *Jesus Prophet of Islam – Revised Edition*, p. 143.

6. Ibid, p. 143.

7. J.A. Robinson, *Barnabas, Hermas and the Didache*, Preface, p. 3.

8. F.C. Conybeare, *The Key of Truth*, p. 91.

9. Ibid, p. 2.

10. Ibid, p. 108.

11. Wallace, *Anti-trinitarian Biographies*, II, p. 117.

12. M. Ata'ur-Rahim and A. Thomson, *Jesus Prophet of Islam – Revised Edition*, p. 158.

13. E. Gibbon, *Decline and Fall of the Roman Empire*, VII, p. 60.

14. Ibid, VI, p. 172.

15. Ibid, VI, p. 173.

16. T. Hodgkin, *Italy and her Invaders*, VI, p. 431.

17. Ibid, VI, p. 431.

18. E. Gibbon, *Decline and Fall of the Roman Empire*, VI, p. 174.

19. Ibid, VI, p. 176.

20. Ibid, VI, p. 179.

21. Ibid, VI, p. 184.

22. Ibid, VI, p. 189.

23. Ibid, VI, p. 179.

24. Ibid, VI, p. 208.

25. Ibid, VI, p. 210.

26. Ibid, VII, p. 57.

27. Ibid, VII, p. 61.

Chapter Nine: The Later Paulicians

1. E. Gibbon, *Decline and Fall of the Roman Empire*, VII, p. 62.

2. Ibid, VII, p. 63.

3. Ibid, VII, p. 68.

4. Ibid, VII, p. 67.

5. Ibid, VII, p. 69.

6. Ibid, VI, p. 64.

7. Ibid, VI, p. 84.

8. Bede, *Ecclesiastical History of the English People*, pp. 307-309.
9. Dr. M. Bucaille, *The Bible, the Qur'an and Science*, p. 67.
10. F.C. Conybeare, *The Key of Truth*, Preface, p. ii.

Chapter Ten: The End of the Paulicians

1. E. Gibbon, *Decline and Fall of the Roman Empire*, IV, p. 395.
2. Ibid, IV, p. 395.
3. H.C. Lea, *A History of the Inquisition*, I, p. 77.
4. M. Ata'ur-Rahim and A. Thomson, *Jesus Prophet of Islam – Revised Edition*, p. 4.
5. Ibid, pp. 149-150.
6. E. Gibbon, *Decline and Fall of the Roman Empire*, VII, p. 385.
7. M. Ata'ur-Rahim and A. Thomson, *Jesus Prophet of Islam – Revised Edition*, p. 151.
8. H.C. Lea, *A History of the Inquisition*, I, p. 154.
9. Ibid, I, p. 154.
10. Ibid, I, p. 129.
11. Ibid, I, p. 299.
12. Ibid, I, p. 328.
13. Ibid, I, p. 328.
14. Ibid, I, p. 283.
15. Ibid, I, p. 296.
16. Ibid, I, p. 296.
17. Ibid, I, p. 294.
18. Ibid, I, p. 321.
19. Ibid, I, p. 226.
20. Ibid, I, p. 339.
21. Ibid, I, p. 347.
22. Ibid, I, p. 450.
23. Ibid, I, p. 459.
24. Ibid, I, p. 541.
25. Ibid, I, p. 85.
26. Ibid, I, p. 101.
27. Ibid, I, p. 101.
28. F.C. Conybeare, *The Key of Truth*, Preface, p. 10.
29. H.C. Lea, *A History of the Inquisition*, I, p. 560.

O   O   O   O   O

Bibliography

The *Qur'an*
The Meaning of the Glorious Qur'an (A translation by
    Muhammad Pickthall), 1930.
The *Hadith* Collections of *Imam* al-Bukhari
    and *Imam* Muslim.
Al-Muwatta' of Imam Malik, (translated by 'A'isha
    'Abdarahman at-Tarjumana and Ya'qub Johnson), 1982.
The *Bible* (King James and New International Versions).

'Abdal-Qadir as-Sufi, *The Way of Muhammad*,
    Diwan Press, 1975.
Professor 'Abdal-Qawi, *Tarikh al-Andalus*.
Ahmad ibn Muhammad (Ibn Idhari), *Al-Bayan al-*
    Maghrib, 1848.
Ali ibn Muhammad, *Annales du Maghreb et de l'Espagne*,
    1898.
Allegro, *The Dead Sea Scrolls*.
Allen, P.S., *Erasmi Epistolai*, 1834 Edn.
Alton, *Religious Opinions of Milton, Locke, and Newton*,
    1833.
Anderson, Norman, *The World's Religions*, 1975.
Apuleius, Lucius, *Metamorphosis - The Golden Ass*, (trans-
    lated by T. Taylor), 1822.
Arpee, L., *The Armenian Awakening*, 1909.
Ata'ur-Rahim, Muhammad, and Thomson, Ahmad,
    Jesus, Prophet of Islam – Revised Edition, 1996.
Augustine, St., *De Civitate Dei*.
Austin, R.J.W., *Sufis of Andalusia*, 1971.

Backwell, R.H., *The Christianity of Jesus*, 1972.
Bainton, R.H., *The Hunted Heretic*, 1953.
Beattie, *The New Theology and the Old*, 1910.
Becker, *The Dead Sea Scrolls*.
Bede, *Ecclesiastical History of the English People*, (edited by
    Bertram Colgrave and R.A.B. Mynors), 1969.
Begin, Menachem, *The Revolt. The Story of the Irgun*,
    (translated by Samuel Karr).

Belloc, J.H.D., *An Open Letter on the Decay of Faith*, 1906.
Bevan, F.R., *Holy Images*, 1940.
Biddle, John, *True Opinion Concerning the Holy Trinity (Twelve Arguments)*, 1653.
Bigg, *The Origin of Christianity*, 1909.
Blackney, E.H., *The Problems of Higher Criticism*, 1905.
Brown, David, *The Structure of the Apocalypse*, 1891.
Brown, W.E., *The Revision of the Prayer Book – A Criticism*, 1909.
Bruce, Frederick, *Jesus and Christian Origins Outside the New Testament*, 1974.
Bruce, F.F., *The New Testament Documents*, 1943.
Bruce, F.F., *The Books and the Parchments*, 1950.
Burch, V., *Myth and Constantine*, 1927.
Burckhardt, T., *Moorish Culture in Spain*, 1972.
Bucaille, Dr. M., *The Bible, the Qur'an and Science*, 4th Edn.
Burnet, Gilbert, *An Abridgement of the History of the Reformation*.
Bury, Arthur, *The Naked Gospel*, 1699.

Carmichael, Joel, *The Death of Jesus*, 1962.
Carnegie, W.H., *Why and What I Believe in Christianity*, 1910.
Carveri, *The Life of Jesus*.
Cary, *Parsons and Pagans – An Indictment of Christianity*, 1906.
Castro, A., *Spaniards, An Introduction to History*, 1971.
Castro, A., *The Structure of Spanish History*, 1954.
Celsus, *Arguments of Celsus* (translated by Lardner), 1830.
Chadwick, H., *Alexandrian Christianity*, 1954.
Chadwick, H., *The Early Church*, 1967.
Channing, W.E., *The Character and Writing of Milton*, 1826.
Channing, W.E., *The Superior Tendency of Unitarianism*, 1831.
Channing, W.E., *The Works of Channing*, 1840-1844.
Chapman, Colin, *Christianity on Trial*, 1974.
Chapman, John, *The Condemnation of Pope Honorius*, 1907.
Charles, R.H., *The Book of Jublilees*, 1917.
Charles, R.H., *The Apocrypha and Pseudo-Epiapapha of the Old Testament*.
Chesterton, G.K., *Orthodoxy*, 1909.

Chillingworth, W., *The Religion of the Protestants*.

Clarke, Samuel, *The Bible*, 1867.

Clodd, Edward, *Gibbon and Christianity*, 1916

Conde, J.A., *The Dominion of the Arabs in Spain*, 1854.

Conybeare, F.J., *Paulicians - the Key to Truth*, 1898.

Cooke, Rev., *Reply to Montgomery*, 1883.

Cooke, Rev., *True to Himself*, 1883.

Corelli, Marie, *Barnabas - A Novel*, 1893.

Corelli, Marie, *Council of Nicea and St. Athanasius*, 1898.

Coulton, G.G., *Sectarian History*, 1937.

Cox, Edwin, *The Elusive Jesus*.

Craver, Marcello, *The Life of Jesus*, 1967.

Cross, *The Oxford Dictionary of Christianity*.

Cross, Frank Moore, *The Ancient Library of Qumran and Modern Biblical Studies*.

Culligan, *The Arian Movement*, 1913.

Cummins, G.D., *The Childhood of Jesus*, 1972.

Cunningham, Francis, *A Dissertation on the Books of Origen Against Celsus*, 1812.

Curll, Edward, *Historical Account of the Life of John Toland*, 1728.

Davies, W.D., *Paul and Rabbinic Judaism*.

De Gayangos, P., *Muhammadan Dynasties in Spain*, 1840.

Dinwiddie, *The Times Before the Reformation*, 1883.

Disciple, *Gospel of the Holy Twelve*.

Doerries, H., *Constantine and Religious Liberty*, 1960.

Doestoevsky, F., *The Brothers Karamazov*, 1933.

Doestoevsky, F., *The Grand Inquisitor*, 1930.

Dozy, R.P.A., *Spanish Islam*.

DuPont-Sommer, *The Jewish Sect of Qumran and the Essenes*, (translated by RD. Barnett).

Duruy, V., *History of Rome*, 1883.

Emlyn, T., *An Humble Enquiry into Scripture*, 1756.

Eusebius, *Church History – Life of Constantine the Great*, (translated by MacGiffert), 1890.

Eusebius, *The Ecclesiastic History*, 1847.

Eusebius, *A Select Library of Nicene and post-Nicene Fathers of the Christian Church*, (translated by A.C. MacGiffert, Ph.D.), 1890.

Everett, C.C., *Theism and the Christian Faith.*

Farrar. P.W., *Early Days of Christianity*, 1898.
Firth, J.B., *Constantine the Great*, 1890.
Frazer, W., *The Golden Bough.*
Frend, W.H.C., *The Early Church.*
Frend, W.H.C., *Persecution in the Early Church.*
Frend, W.H.C., *An Address to the Inhabitants of Cambridge,* 1788.
Frend, W.H.C., *The Rise of the Monophysite Movement.*
Frend, W.H.C., *Coulthurst's Blunders Exposed*, 1788-89.
Frend, W.H.C., *The Donatist Church.*
Froude, *The Life and Letters of Erasmus*, 1916.

Gannett, D., *Francis David, Founder of Unitarianism*, 1914.
Gibbon, Edward, *Christianity*, 1930.
Gibbon, Edward, *Decline and Fall of the Roman Empire,* 1823, 1909-1914.
Gibson, J.M., *Inspiration and Authority of the Holy Scriptures.*
Glover, T.R., *Jesus of History*, 1919.
Goodspeed, E.J., *The Letter of Barnabas*, 1950.
Goodspeed, E.J., *The Apostolic Fathers*, 1950.
Gordon, Alexander, *Heresy.*
Grant & Fridman, *The Secret Sayings of Jesus*, 1960.
Graves, K., *The World's Sixteen Crucified Saviours*, 1881.
Green, *Sir Isaac Newton's Views*, 1871.
Guignebert, C., *Jesus*, 1935.
Guthrie, D., *A Shorter Life of Christ*, 1970.
Gwatkin, *Arius.*

Haines, *Religious Persecution.*
Hall, L, *The Continuity of Revelation*, 1908.
Harnack, Adolf, *Christianity and History*, (translated by Saunders), 1900.
Harnack, Adolf, *Outlines of the History of Dogma*, 1900.
Harnack, Adolf, *What is Christianity?*, 1901.
Harris, J.R., *Celsus and Aristedes*, 1921.
Harwood, P., *Priestly and Unitarianism*, 1842.
Hastings, *Dictionary of Christ and the Gospel.*
Hay, J.S., *Heliogabalus*, 1911.

Haygood, A.G., *The Monk and the Prince*, 1895.

Hayne, S., *The General View of the Holy Scripture*, 1607.

Heinimann, *John Toland*, 1944.

Hermes, *Hermes – A Disciple of Jesus*, 1888.

Hodgkin, T., *Italy and Her Invaders*.

Holzmann, Heinrich, *Lebuch II*.

Hone, W., *The Apocryphal New Testament*, 1820.

Hort, F.J.A., *Six Lectures on the Ante-Nicene Fathers*, 1895.

Huddleston, *Toland's History of the Druids*, 1814.

Hunt, *Jesus Christ*, 1904.

Hussain, Iftekhar Bano, *Prophets in the Qur'an, Volume Two: The Later Prophets*, 1995.

Hynes, S., *The Manifesto*, 1697.

Ibn Kathir, *The Signs before the Day of Judgement*, (translated by Huda Khattab), 1991.

Imammudin, *A Political History of Muslim Spain*, 1969.

Irving, T., *The Falcon of Spain*, 1973.

Jan, *John Hus - His Life*, 1915.

Jones, A.H.M., *Constantine and the Conversion of Europe*, 1948.

Josephus, *The Works of Flavius Josephus*, (translated by William Whitson), 1840.

Joyce, D., *The Jesus Scroll*, 1973.

Kamen, H.A.R., *The Spanish Inquisition*, 1965.

Kaye, J., *The Council of Nicea*, 1853.

Kaye, J., *The Ecclesiastic History of the 2nd & 3rd Centuries*, 1893.

Kaye, J., *The Sermons*, 1850.

Kaspary, J., *The Life of the Real Jesus*, 1904.

Kaspary, J., *The Origin, Growth, and Decline of Christianity*, 1904-10.

Kelly, J.N.D., *Early Christian Creeds*, 1949.

Khan, M.Z., *The Gardens of the Righteous*, 1975.

Kingsley, C., *Hypathia*.

Kirkgaldy, *The New Theology and the Old*, 1910.

Knight, *The Life of Faustus Socianus*, (translated by Biddle), 1653.

Knox, W.L., *The Sources of the Synoptic Gospels*, 1953.

Konstantinides, *Saint Barnabas*, 1971.

Lardner, N., *A History of Heretics*, 1780.
Lardner, N., *Two Schemes of Trinity*, 1829.
Laurence, C.E., *The Wisdom of the Apocrypha*, 1910.
Latourette, K.C., *A History of the Expansion of Christianity*, 1953.
Lea, H.C., *Chapters from the Religious History of Spain*, 1890.
Lea, H.C., *The Church of Rome*, 1892.
Lea, H.C., *The Inquisition, its Organization and Operation*, 1954.
Lea, H.C., *A History of the Inquisition*, 1888.
Lea, H.C., *A History of the Inquisition in Spain*, 1906.
Lea, H.C., *The Inquisition in Spanish Dependencies*, 1954.
Lea, H.C., *The Moriscos of Spain*, 1901.
Leany, A.R.C., *The Dead Sea Scrolls*.
Leany, A.R.C., *The Rule of Qumran*.
Le Clerc, *The Apostolic Fathers*.
Leff, G.A., *Mediaeval Thought*, 1959.
Lehman, Johannes, *The Jesus Report*, 1972.
Lietzman, Hanz, *The Beginning of the Christian Church*, 1949.
Lietzman, Hanz, *A History of the Early Church*, 1961.
Lindsey, T., *Two Dissertations*, 1779.
Lindsey, T., *An Historical View of the State of Unitarian Doctrine*, 1783.
Lindsey, T., *A List of False Readings of the Scripture*, 1790.
Lubinietski, *A History of the Reformation in Poland*.

MacGiffert, A.C., *The Apostles' Creed*, 1902.
MacGiffert, A.C., *The God of the Early Christians*, 1924.
MacGiffert, A.C., *A History of Christianity in the Apostolic Age*, 1897.
MacLachlan, *The Religious Opinions of Milton, Locke, and Newton*, 1941.
Madden, *Life and Martyrdom of Savonarola*, 1854.
Major, John, *'Sentences'*.
Marshall, G.N., *Challenge of a Liberal Faith*, 1966.
Marshall, G.N., *Understanding of Albert Schweitzer*, 1966.
Masters, John, *Baptismal Vows, or the Feast of St. Barnabas*, 1866.

Mellone, S.H., *Unitarianism and the New Theology*, 1908.

Menendez-Pilal, R., *The Cid and his Spain*, 1934.

Miller, F., *The History of the Jewish People in the Age of Jesus Christ*.

Milton, J., *Treatise of Civil Power*.

Milton, J., *The Christian Doctrine*, 1825.

Motley, *Rise of the Dutch Republic*.

Mowry, Lucetta, *The Dead Sea Scrolls and the Early Church*.

Murray, G.G.A., *Five Stages of Greek Religion*.

Nadawi, *Tarikh al-Andalus*.

Naser, A., *Tarikh al-Hispania*.

Newman, A., *Jesus* (with a Preface by Dr. Schmeidal), 1907.

Newman, Cardinal, *Apologia*, 1913.

Newman, F.W., *Christianity in its Cradle*, 1884.

Newman, F.W., *Hebrew Jesus*, 1895.

Newman, F.W., *The Historical Depravity of Christianity*, 1871.

Newman, J.H., *Arianism of the Fourth Century*, 1833.

Newton, *Sir Isaac Newton Daniel*, 1922.

Orwell, G., *'1984'*.

Oxyrhynchus, *New Sayings of Jesus and Fragments of a Lost Gospel*, (translated by B.P. Grenfell & A.S. Hunt), 1897.

Parke, D.B., *The Epic of Unitarianism*, 1957.

Patrick, John, *The Apology of Origen in Reply to Celsus*, 1892.

Pike, E.R., *Spiritual Basis of Nonconformity*, 1897.

Pike, J.A., *If This Be Heresy*, 1967.

Pike, J.A., *Time for Christian Candour*, 1965.

Pike, J.A., *The Wilderness Revolt*, 1972.

Prescott, W., *History of Charles V*, 1905.

Priestly, Joseph, *A General History of the Christian Church*, 1802.

Priestly, Joseph, *A History of the Corruption of Christianity*, 1871.

Priestly, Joseph, *History of Jesus Christ*, 1786.

Priestly, Joseph, *Memoirs of Dr. Priestly*, 1904.

Priestly, Joseph, *Socrates and Jesus*, 1803.

Priestly, Joseph, *Three Tracts*, 1791.
Priestly, Joseph, *Dr. Priestly's Catechism*, 1796.
Priestly, Joseph, *A New Song*, 1876.
Puccinelli, P., *Vita de S. Barnaba Apostolo.*

Quick, Murid, *The Story of Barnabas.*

Ragg, Lonsdale and Laura, *The Gospel of Barnabas,*
    (edited and translated from the Italian Ms.
    in the Imperial Library at Vienna), 1921.
Reed, Douglas, *The Controversy of Zion*, 1985.
Reland, Adrian, *Historical and Critical Reflections upon
    Mohametanism and Socianism*, 1712.
Reland, Adrian, *Treatises concerning the Mohametons.*
Rendall, *The Theology of Hebrew Christians*, 1886.
Rice, D.T., *Byzantine Art*, 1954.
Rice, Michael, *False Inheritance*, 1994.
Robertson, D.D., *Charles V, Emperor*, 1798.
Robinson, J.A., *Barnabas, Hermas and the Didache*, 1920.
Robinson, J.A.T., *Honest to God*, 1964.
Robinson, J.M., *The New Quest of the Historical Jesus*, 1959.
Robinson, J.M., *Problem of History in Mark*, 1957.
Robertson, J .M., *The Historical Jesus*, 1916.
Robson, Rev. James, *Christ in Islam*, 1929.
Ruinus, *Commentary on the Apostles' Creed*, 1955.
Runciman, S., *The Fall of Constantinople*, 1965.
Runciman, S., *History of the Crusades*, 1965.
Rylcy, G.B., *Barnabas, or the Great Renunciation*, 1893.

Sanday, *Outlines of the Life of Christ.*
Sandmel, S., *We Jews and Jesus*, 1973.
Santucci, L., *Wrestling with Jesus*, 1972.
Savonarola, *Verity of Christian Faith*, 1651.
Schmiedel, P.W., *Jesus in Modern Criticism*, 1907.
Schokel, L.A., *Understanding Biblical Research*, 1968.
Schweitzer, Albert, *Christianity and the Religions
    of the World*, 1923.
Schweitzer, Albert, *The Mysticism of Paul the Apostle*,
    1953.
Schweitzer, Albert, *Paul and his Interpreters.*
Schweitzer, Albert, *The Kingdom of God and Primitive
    Christianity*, 1968.

Schweitzer, Albert, *The Philosophy of Civilization*, 1946.
Schweitzer, Albert, *A Psychiatric Study of Jesus*, 1958.
Schweitzer, Albert, *The Story of Albert Schweitzer*.
Scott, C.A.A., *Ulfilas, Apostle of the Goths*.
Sedillot, L.P.E.A., *Histoire des Arabs*, 1850.
Socretes, *Ecclesiastical History*, 1845.
Sox, David, *The Gospel of Barnabas*, 1984.
Sozomenus, *Ecclesiastical History*, 1890.
Spark, *Unitarian Miscellany*.
Spark, *Christian Reformer*.
Stanley, A.P., *The Eastern Church*, 1869.
Stanley, A.P., *The Athanasian Creed*, 1871.
Stanley, A.P., *Lectures on the History of the Eastern Church*, 1883.
Stevenson, J., *Creeds, Councils, and Controversies*.
Stevenson, J., *Studies in Eusebius*, 1929.
Stevenson, J., *The New Eusebius*.

Taylor, John, *The Scriptural Doctrine of Original Sin*.
Taylor, John, *A History of the Octagon Church*.
Thomas-a-Kempis, *Imitation of Christ*, (translated by John Wesley), 1903.
Thompson, F.A., *Goths in Spain*, 1969.
Thomson, A., *The Next World Order*, 1994.
Throop, P., *A Criticism of the Crusades*, 1940.
Toland, John, *History of the Druids*, 1740.
Toland, John, *Hypathia*, 1753.
Toland, John, *The Nazarenes*, 1718.
Toland, John, *Theological and Philosophical Works*, 1732.
Toland, John, *Tetradymus*.
Towgood, *Serious and Free Thoughts on the Present State of the Church*.

Vermas, G., *Jesus, the Jew*, 1973.
Vos, J.G., *A Christian Introduction to Religions of the World*, 1965.

Wallace, *Anti-trinitarian Biographies*, 1850.
Warchaurr, J., *Jesus or Christ?*, 1909.
Warfield, B.B., *Jesus or Christ?*, 1909.
Whittaker, T., *The Origins of Christianity*, 1933.

Wilbur, E.M., *A History of Unitarianism in Transylvania, England, and America.*

Williamson, G.A., *The History of the Church*, 1965.

Williamson, G.A., *The Jewish War*, 1959.

Wilson, E.M., *The Dead Sea Scrolls*, 1969.

Wisaart, H.S., *Socialism and Christ, the Great Enemy of the Human Race*, 1905.

Workman, H.B., *Persecution in the Early Church*, 1906.

Workman, H.B., *Martyrs of the Early Church*, 1913.

Zahn, T., *The Articles of the Apostles' Creed*, 1899.

Zahn, T., *Introduction to the New Testament*, 1909.

Zahn, T., *Peter, Saint and Apostle*, 1889.

Periodicals

Christian Examiner, Jan. 1924-Dec. 1925.

Edinburgh Review, Vol. XII, 1825.

Hibbert Journal Supplement, *Jesus or Christ*, Vol. VII, 1909.

Harvard Theological Review, *Theism and the Christian Faith*, 1909.

Islamic Horizons, Feb. 1985, *Today's Gospel of Barnabas – Is it Authentic?*

Neale, Samuel, *A select series of biographical narratives, etc.*, Vol. VIII, 1845.

Review Biblique, 1950.

Sunday Times, Weekly Review, 10th April 1977.

Time Magazine, May 24, 1976.

About the Authors

Muhammad Ata'ur-Rahim lived much of his life in Hyderabad, India, before moving to Pakistan at the time of the Partition in 1947. He was awarded the degrees of BT, LLB and MA at the Muslim University of Aligarh, before completing his further studies in education at the Universities of Edinburgh and London, where he was awarded his MRST. He was the Government of India Scholar in the Archaeology, Art and Religion of Ancient India. After being promoted to the rank of Colonel during the Second World War, in which he served with distinction, Muhammad Ata'ur-Rahim became the Principal of the Urdu College in Karachi, Pakistan. His other books include *Unitarianism in Christianity* and *The Meeting Ground of Islam and Christianity*. He died in 1978, *'alehi rahma*.

Ahmad Thomson was born in Chipata, Zambia, on the 23rd of April, 1950, towards the end of the British colonial period in Africa. Educated in both Zimbabwe and England, and widely travelled, he was fortunate enough to escape having too rigid a cultural moulding or social conditioning, and accordingly, although brought up as a Christian, recognised and embraced Islam for what it is when he encountered it, clearly and existentially embodied by real Muslims.

Soon after embracing Islam, the author met Colonel Muhammad Ata'ur-Rahim, who had come to England in order to pursue his studies of Jesus, peace be upon him, and Christianity in greater depth, and at the suggestion of Shaykh 'Abd al-Qadir al-Murabit they began to work together. As a result of their joint research three books were written, *Jesus, Prophet of Islam, Jesus in Qur'an*, and *Blood on the Cross* which was completed after the author had been on pilgrimage to Makka and after Colonel Rahim had died, *'alehi rahma*.

Other books written by Ahmad Thomson include *Dajjal - The King who has no clothes*, which is a contemporary study of the Anti-Christ written from a Qur'anic perspective and based on some of the recorded sayings of the Prophet Muhammad, may the blessings and peace of Allah be on him and his family and his Companions and all who follow him and them in what they are able with sincerity until the Last Day. Amin.